THE DESIGNER'S GUIDE TO PRODUCT VISION

LEARN TO BUILD YOUR STRATEGIC INFLUENCE TO SHAPE THE FUTURE

LAURA FISH | SCOTT KIEKBUSCH

New Riders

VOICES THAT MATTER™

The Designer's Guide to Product Vision
Learn to build your strategic influence to shape the future

Laura Fish and Scott Kiekbusch

Voices That Matter
www.voicesthatmatter.com
San Francisco, CA

Voices That Matter is an imprint of Pearson Education, Inc.
To report errors, please send a note to errata@peachpit.com

Executive Editor: Laura Norman
Development Editor: Margaret S. Anderson
Senior Production Editor: Tracey Croom
Copy Editor: Liz Welch
Compositor: Kim Scott, Bumpy Design
Proofreader: Becky Winter
Indexer: Valerie Haynes Perry
Cover Design: Chuti Prasertsith and Laura Fish
Interior Design: Kim Scott, Bumpy Design

ISBN-13: 978-0-13-665432-2
ISBN-10: 0-13-665432-0

1 2020

*To designers who stand where we once stood:
wanting to find a better way forward for their
contributions, their career, and their profession.*

ACKNOWLEDGMENTS

Special thanks to our Peachpit executive editor Laura Norman, who had a vision for our vision about product vision. And our development editor Margaret Anderson, who stewarded us through the process and was our steadfast cheerleader. We would also like to thank the many people who over the years helped us along the way, and to those who have been dedicated to this project, helping make it all happen.

The Wholesome Medley Crew:

> Ami Brenner
> Amanda Hegge
> Luke Flynt
> Kevin Sawyer
> Cory Madaris
> Shawn Vallereux
> Audrey Cahill
> Christian Hurley
> Mike Gaines

. . . and before Wholesome Medley, Paul Sullivan

For their insightful interview answers:

> Jason Goodwin
> Chisara Nwabara
> Martin Ringlein
> Chris Whitlock

The Peachpit team:

> Laura Norman
> Margaret S. Anderson
> Tracey Croom
> Elizabeth Welch
> Kim Scott
> Chuti Prasertsith
> Becky Winter

Laura would like to thank...

Scott, for partnering with me on another design adventure—getting him to agree is always just a matter of how much time it will take to wear him down; my uncle, Dr. Michael Peter Shepley, who showed me by example what it takes to go after big visions and the importance of nurturing creativity; and, most importantly, my parents and my sisters, Steph and Merry, for their love and unwavering support.

Scott would like to thank...

Laura for dragging me kicking and screaming into this book writing endeavor; Scott Granneman for providing me with my introduction to the field of web design and development at Washington University; and, above all, my wife Valerie Knopik, for her unconditional support, patience, and love.

CONTENTS

PART I: THE CALLING

PART II: THE VISION

6 Telling the Story of the Future Experience — 140

PART III: VISIONEERING

7 Setting Your Compass to the North Star   178

PREFACE

RITE OF PASSAGE

I'm a quirky creative—someone whose reality is only *slightly* augmented by an overactive imagination, and a junkie for those highs that come with the spark of a promising idea. Layer on top of that, I set high standards for myself, and by extension, those with whom I work. Admittedly, I have to check myself at times. I channel my nonconformist nature to challenge status quo thinking and inspire change. While my intentions are always good, that nonconformity has led to my losing jobs. I learn big lessons the hard way but am always optimistic about the future. I know what I'm made of, what I'm capable of, and what I stand for. Thankfully, these qualities have helped to elevate me professionally as a designer and serve vision work well.

I'm passionate about creating visions. I have been fortunate, for the entirety of my career, to be able to do just that. At each past job, I entered a company to fill a predefined tactical role. It would only take weeks—once hours—to break free of my designated box. Like a heat-seeking missile, I could see how to move what existed in the present into tomorrow's bigger picture possibilities. I'd find value where no one else was bothering to look, illuminate experience cracks begging to be filled, inspiring everyone from my peers to the CEO with my innovation-minded vision proposals. As long as I completed my weekly list of tactical responsibilities, I was granted the privilege of working on vision proposals as a side hustle.

Of course, the difference between my visions at the beginning of my career and those of recent years was—of course—strategic viability. In hindsight, my earliest vision work as a young professional didn't have a chance of becoming real offerings. I was naive to think so. As I matured with professional experience, I became more invested in seeing my vision work actually make it to real users.

In 2014, I was fortunate to find a stellar partner-in-design (crime) and mentor to work with: Scott Kiekbusch. Together, albeit unknowingly, we embarked on a design pilgrimage that would be a transformative experience—especially for me. Our partnership clarified how, as a designer, I could better make use of my innate skills. Then together, we learned how to harness strategic thinking to drive bigger, better vision work.

Our journey began at a large company on its highest-profile, most visionary endeavor: figure out what was next, beyond its long-standing flagship offering. This ask was right up my alley. At the time, I was a decade into my career. I had established myself in Boston as someone who could straighten out a tangled mess to visualize tomorrow's big-picture possibility. I also had a preference to work as a sole contributor (a bit diva like, I know). This project would be the first time I was officially paired with a design partner. Scott meet Laura, Laura meet Scott. I'd eventually learn the importance of creatives working in pairs, but at the time—as we were completely consumed with this mega project—I was just thankful I wasn't in it alone.

From the get-go, the work was in constant jeopardy of catastrophic collapse. The chaos was caused by all the usual suspects: impossibly demanding stakeholders, business stepping on design, design stepping on business. And all the while our gung-ho development team frantically coding with no strategic plan in sight. The stress was off the charts, leaving a trail of casualties and panic attacks in its massive wake. But what was unique about the project was the setup: absolute collaboration and co-location. Our continuous, close proximity afforded us the opportunity to regularly work within a few feet of the assigned digital business strategists.

Scott first recognized the potential of a closer design-business alliance and persuaded me that this was the better way forward. For the greater part of the year, he and I worked tirelessly to pull down the barriers that persisted between our team's business associates and designers. The commitment paid off. Narrowing the gap helped ease the discord. It was a small miracle. As our two disciplines gelled, we learned to collaboratively make decisions. I also learned to be wiser at choosing my battles on behalf of design.

At some point between working lunches and trust falls, Scott and I were granted total visibility through the business wall—a rare opportunity to see the motivations and intricacies of the working business strategy. Understanding the factors driving the business decisions helped the two of us to further elevate how we tackled design.

Going forward, we would deliberately integrate the needs of the user with the wants of the company, aiming to solve for user problems with business objectives top of mind. The importance of this business-designer relationship made a lasting impression on me. I even toyed with the idea of enrolling in business school for a hot minute in an effort to combat my newly discovered business illiteracy. But ultimately, I settled on home schooling myself to learn the basics of business. My goal was to be able to have an intelligent conversation with my business peers, and that meant being able to speak the language of business. The success of that high-profile effort was a realization that designers should be working with our strategic business counterparts not as adversaries but *as partners*.

Another big win was that Scott recognized the need to define our work efforts in concise, articulate statements—no more vague, lengthy monologues. He began using a simple problem statement formula that proved wildly successful. With all of the newly acquired insights, we constructed a thoughtful, comprehensive, problem-focused process—the design-business partnership woven into every stage. Our aim was to leverage design thinking to craft tactical solutions with user problems squarely rooted in the needs of the business. And...it was working for us.

Scott and I presented our process several times to hundreds of people within the firm—and gained a following of colleague-fans. We had gone viral. We were models for this new approach to digital product work. So, we pushed our luck and went for it: an ultimatum.

For our new process to truly be effective, both sides of the partnership needed to be on equal footing. We asked that, going forward, designers and our product business associates work at the same hierarchical level. Although inspired by our example, the business associates refused to relinquish their carte blanche power and grant equal weight in decision making to design team members. Fortunately, our special small group remained the exception. Unfortunately, the majority of the projects around us continued to suffer from design/business inequalities.

Fast-forward another year—and several nervous breakdowns later—Scott and I had a major breakthrough. The years of accumulated visioning exercises had started to look like a pile of related puzzle pieces, finally revealing a path toward an innovative solution. And the research backed us up. Our visionary digital product idea would move this mega company from its dinosaur legacy status to the head of the class. This product had the potential to truly better people's lives, and on an enterprise platform, that meant impact on a really massive scale. Stakeholders granted us the go-ahead to create a proof of concept.

The green light was as exciting as it was terrifying. Most internal innovation efforts seem fated to unfold in the same way: an optimistic start, followed by an increasingly rocky middle stage, and an execution process that drags on and on to a slow death. We were desperate to cheat fate and help our fledgling product reach market.

Leveraging a strategic mindset, hell-bent determination, and a shared nonconformist nature, we found our footing with a well-thought-out plan. The first move was to assemble a talented team made up of bold, strategic thinkers from all corners of the digital product space. Once our core team was in place, we tapped specialized industry experts to be on standby.

Out of the gate, we preemptively assured leadership that all the boxes were checked. Business goals, check. Validated user problems, check. Technology...eh, kinda check? (As it turns out, artificial intelligence is more complicated than our engineers would admit.) We then roughly translated the visionary idea into realistic near-term goals while acknowledging our longer-term aspirations.

To sign off, leadership had but one final request. They asked me to "quickly" mockup high fidelity visual designs of the idea. I politely declined. But the stakeholders weren't comfortable allocating more funding until they had something tangible—something they could wrap their eyes around. To placate them, I leveraged a unique take on storytelling to express the high-level intentions of our idea without getting into specific features or detailed designing. It worked. We were off and running...and then, we weren't.

In fairness, this massive project had made huge strides. Our solution accounted for the business wants and user needs and was a strong contender to dominate an emerging market position. We had launched a minimal valuable product (MVP), successfully testing with a sizable base of established customers, and our team continued to launch iterative releases. The project's undoing would end up being the same reason the effort was celebrated: it was different. Very different. Although this incredible product truly represented the *desired* path forward for the company, it didn't align well with their current mission. Looking back, it was a huge mistake. To include our product as an expanded offering, the powers that be would have to alter the company's raison d'être—the mission and purpose—which meant reshuffling the legacy offerings to share that coveted top spot. But those legacy offerings were the company's main cash cow. Leadership found themselves paralyzed, incapable of making any decisions that could rock their steady money boat. Death by indecision. Fate had finally tracked us down.

Although we didn't get to see the ultimate vision of our game-changing digital product make it to primetime, I'm grateful for the opportunities that led to an invaluable surge of professional growth. But while growing by leaps and bounds, those years were insanely difficult. Challenging the status quo is not only exhausting, it's professionally treacherous (but I already knew that). It wasn't until I was finally out of the thick of things, licking my wounds and reflecting on my experiences as a whole, that I could see the bigger picture.

Over the course of time Scott and I worked together, I learned to shed my go-to pixel-based habits and expanded outward from an exclusive focus on near-term tactical output. With Scott's help (and his infinite well of patience), I leapfrogged from a designer who presented her thoughts via screen mockups to becoming articulately strategic about my design decisions. At this point in time, with a better grasp of business basics, I had become the bridge that connected design to business. And with an evolved product game and strategic maturity, I now understood how to better realize digital product offerings. I also had witnessed something I hadn't seen before—a designer, Scott, be accepted as a partner by our senior business partner; he was akin to a co-captain of the larger operation.

I had a newfound professional purpose that anchored my innate talents in work that was positively impacting the world. And at the heart of it all was my love for big, bold vision. Our work helped me articulate that strategy-led product vision is the keystone of any product or service. Importantly, product vision had to be fused with solid strategy from the start, and those strategic threads had to be pulled through every sprint. Scott and I truly harnessed our power as strategic designers. I called this new strategic take on product vision for an agile world, Visioneering. Fitting, no?

After years of developing, clarifying and refining the thinking, Scott and I are sharing it all in *The Designer's Guide to Product Vision*. It was a labor of love for design. I'm proud to be helping fellow designers and will be here to help tactical designers, like myself once, embark on their own pilgrimage to become strategic. But more than anything, I will be excited to see strategic designers collectively harness our newfound power with bold visions to shape big real-world change for the better. Because the world needs big change, and who better than the designer to help lead the charge to make that happen. Who's with me?

Laura Fish
May 2020

FEATURES IN THIS BOOK

 ## INTERVIEWS: DESIGNING FROM INSIDE THE BOX

To help the designer see themselves succeeding in this role, look through-out the book for "Designing from Inside the Box" features, interviews with industry design pros who are walking the walk and talking about how they express product vision and strategy in their practice to find success in established business.

TRY IT THIS WAY

The Visioneering framework allows teams the freedom to customize it with their own resources. So, bring your own arsenal of preferred tactical processes, flows, and exercises to support your Visioneering efforts—screen-level designing processes, systems, problem statement formats, sketching exercises, design thinking flows, scrum variations, and organizing standards.

Throughout the book, you'll see a mile-marker icon designating "Try It This Way" callouts. Look to these for our recommendations on specific ways that have worked for us.

➡ TRY IT THIS WAY

As part of the larger design community, keep your finger on the pulse of which tactical processes and resources are developing, and which new trends are worthy of consideration. Look to peer-to-peer articles and forums to crowd-source opinions on what's working versus what's not. As your Visioneering team matures, so will your arsenal. What will develop is a truly mindful, flexible, and collaborative way of approaching the ask.

THE DESIGNER'S DECLARATION

Let's call it how it is: business has yet to recognize design as a core competency. In turn, without that seat at the table, designers aren't positioned (or encouraged) to reach their full potential. Suffice it to say, this situation is hurting both business and design.

Trust that we designers have a higher calling. Answering that call forces us to reclaim the discipline of design and redefine it for modern times. Ours will be the modern era of design. Practitioners are called upon to be skilled in defining not only form and function, but *strategy*—designers leveraging their highly creative lens to assemble connections via skillful problem solving. With this new platform, designers can sculpt the inevitable: change—a gift that bears a weighty responsibility. We must use this gift to its fullest extent and effect change only for *better*.

The modern era of design will bring a revolutionary shift that will not only transform designers, but also guarantee them a seat at the grownup table. This shift will also trigger the product space to rearrange and unify—this unification looks like design, engineering, and business comprehensively integrating to mindfully craft the best *experience* for the user. Going forward, experience is the highest guiding tenet. We are witnessing the beginning of the designer leading the charge.

To achieve this level of leadership, the designer working on user experience teams must first advance from a *tactical* designer to a *strategic* designer. Only when this hard-won transformation is complete can the designer harness their newfound power, and they do that by taking the lead to create innovative product visions and high-level involvement in their realization.

It's all about the product vision. As the keystone of any product or service, the job of a product vision is to explain a strategy's complex connections and express the product's future intended destination. This can be done by telling the story of an experience and conceptually illustrating the offering's intentions, without getting into detailed designing.

When the team is ready to translate all of that innovative thinking from the product vision into tangible output, how exactly do they do that? It's fair to say, this is where most product development programs get tripped up because programs are working solely against a product roadmap (or simply a laundry list of features). Know that today every product or service journey is an uncharted expedition. Now more than ever the landscape is unpredictable—quick to change due to the fast-paced nature of technology and ever-rising bar of user expectation. What the team sees in front of them today, may soon shift—rendering product roadmaps obsolete. To navigate this terrain, Visioneering is the navigational tool we use to implement our product vision while keeping in alignment with the North Star (the company's mission & purpose). The product now bound to a purposeful direction, as the team iteratively and continuously delivers the best experience that meets the needs of both the business and the target audience.

By way of the product vision and Visioneering, the strategic designer has the means to not only course-correct the wayward business ship, but also ultimately influence its direction. Positioning the designer to lead today's slated projects and shape tomorrow's bigger picture. It's all about ingenuity, creativity, and the smart approach to iteratively execute.

Through this book, we plan to show you exactly how to make that happen.

PART I
THE CALLING

You've heard the call. Part I clarifies the importance of product vision and why you, the designer, are suited to strategically lead that work. Then it walks you step-by-step through transforming your role from a focus on tactical design deliverables to a strategic designer.

- Learn high-level talking points that make an ironclad case for product vision.

- Develop superior communication and facilitation skills, and master a handful of techniques to collaboratively lead product vision endeavors.

- Tactfully challenge assumptions and begin mastering first principles thinking.

CHAPTER 1

THE STATE
OF THE DESIGNER

Let's call it how it is: the majority of businesses have yet to recognize design—a proven competitive advantage in today's marketplace—as a core competency. In turn, without that seat at the table, designers aren't in a place to influence leadership decisions or positioned (or encouraged) to reach their full potential, causing the discipline of design to idle. Suffice to say, this is hurting both business and design.

As designers, our struggle to be seen as more than tactical resources is real. Very real. But it hasn't deterred us—in fact, the opposite is true. Determination to prove our worth and that of design has gotten fiercer. However, we can't continue to try to move the needle individually, in a vacuum. To achieve success, we designers must unite under a shared mission, define a universal means for advancement, and organize the movement to claim our rightful position as strategic leaders. All signs point to this being the time for that revolution.

Designers intuitively trust that our profession is destined for a higher calling. Answering that call will require us to first reclaim the discipline of design and then redefine it for modern times. As it stands today, the accepted role of the designer is to define aesthetics (what it looks like) and identify potential usability concerns. We're often viewed solely as decorators responsible for delivering a superficial layer of a product. This isolates design at the tactical end of the project funnel. By this definition, design is purely reactive and tactically focused. Design's greater contribution includes—or should include—the work at the beginning of the funnel, helping to assemble strategy. This is modern-era design. Practitioners of modern-era design are called on to be skilled in defining not only form and function, but *strategy* as well. Designers adept at modern-era design leverage their highly creative lenses to assemble connections via skillful problem solving. With this new platform, designers can envision and create the future—a gift that bears a weighty responsibility. We must use this gift to its fullest extent and effect change only for the *better*.

The champion of modern-era design is the strategic designer. But design will have to earn its seat at the strategic table. It will take a track record of success for businesses to see the greater worth of design, and by extension the greater worth of the design practitioner, beyond what is currently universally defined and accepted.

You may decide focusing solely on the tactical aesthetic route is the right path for your design career. That may be enough for you, and that is perfectly okay. However, if you want to be at the forefront of creating the product vision—and be a core member of the *Visioneering* leadership team driving its implementation—then you must be strategic. That means becoming conversant with the business side of things.

In this chapter we'll introduce the role of the strategic designer, explain the difference between tactics and strategy, and assert the designer's central function in establishing a product vision. We'll take a brief look at the history of the product designer and consider employment options for the powerful role of strategic designer. Finally, we'll introduce the two processes central to this book: the product vision and Visioneering.

STRATEGY VS. TACTICS

To help clarify the difference between strategy and tactics, we'll turn to the tried-and-true sports analogy. The head coach of a football team is responsible for developing a strategy to win a game (winning games being the goal of the team, obviously). To do this, the coach will research the strengths and weaknesses of the opposing team. After developing a solid understanding of their opponent as well as the skills of their own players, the coach will develop a high-level game plan (strategy). For instance, our research tells us that the opposing team's quarterback completely falls apart under pressure. In other words, when the opposing team's defenders get close to the quarterback, he gets rattled. The coach's strategy applies that knowledge by designing a game plan that puts considerable pressure on the quarterback with frequent blitzes (i.e. sending one or more additional defensive players to attack the quarterback).

Understanding the head coach's "pressure the quarterback" strategy, the defensive coaches and players develop the specific plays (tactics) used on the field to do just that. Plays include staying close to the opposing team's receivers with man-to-man coverage and applying extra pressure on the quarterback. Then, in real time during the game, the tactics are evaluated and adjusted based on how well they're observed to be working. If it's clear that the tactics are failing, it's time to revisit the strategy. The same is true for product strategy.

Well-conceived product strategy surfaces and identifies the right dots that will be continuously connected via the tactics in order to achieve business outcomes. *The success and failure of individual tactics are the yardstick of a winning strategy.* Memorize that line; it slays every time.

A DEMANDING JOURNEY

Here's the fine print: it won't be easy. Most designers working as sole contributors or members of a product design team are predominantly tactical designers—at the lowest rung of the ladder, tethered to the pixel deliverables and respective usability. Not exactly what we envisioned for ourselves as proud architects of the user experience. Advancing from tactical designer to strategic designer is a demanding journey to get to the promised land.

Not sure the strategic route is for you? Accruing expertise in the complexities of strategy and underlying discipline of business may seem overwhelming. No worries; it's not for every designer. Those who choose to remain as tactical designers fill a crucial role. Not only is the work defining the topmost layer of a product valuable, it's also incredibly time consuming. No decent art director will underestimate the dense hours that go into defining a comprehensive visual language. But here's the ask: elevate your tactical efforts beyond just defining, to contribute more making. Just as the strategic designer will have to become the bridge that connects design to business, in the same way, the tactical designer must be the bridge that connects design to engineering: the *elevated* tactical designer.

Not too long ago, the designer doubled as both the definer and maker. Circa Y2K, the web designer's job responsibilities included front-end web development. The front end was less complex back then—most designers were up and coding in no time. And yes, this was a disparaging of design. We were required to code because design was deemed far less valuable than engineering contributions. Nevertheless, this is the right idea—an interface concept spec'd out in Sketch is just theory until the CSS is built and tested. This requires the designer to have a good understanding of not only the pixels but also how to implement them on the screen. In the digital space, this means brushing up on front-end development basics. Think CSS, JavaScript, and the fundamentals of cross-browser compatibility. The developer you pair with, iterating on-screen specs in real time, will thank you.

Over time, as an elevated tactical designer with a daily scrum schedule that keeps the two disciplines closely intertwined, you'll learn to make all the right moves to function as the bridge that connects design to engineering. You'll be familiar with the basics of front-end code, and you'll have nurtured your logical thinking skills and practiced putting objectivity in front of subjectivity. Because of this, the elevated tactical designer is the best candidate to level up to strategic designer when ready.

For those designers who are ready to come along for the ride, the transformation from tactical designer to strategic designer is revealed, step-by-step, in Chapter 2, "re-Design School." And once your place as a fully-fledged strategic designer is earned, then comes the good stuff. Harnessing that newfound power through the keystone of a product or service: product vision.

Trust that now is the best time for designers to fulfill our professional destinies. It's progress that's been 45 years in the making. Marking a long-awaited coming of age. Let's take a gander at how strategic designers arrived at this moment...we have a theory.

HISTORY LESSON

The designer's family tree winds through centuries of artistry, craftsmanship, and industry to eventually extend a new branch into the digital age. There in the pixels of the 1980s, at innovative companies like Xerox, Microsoft, and Apple, traditional software architecture and the business of technology began to deliberately fuse with the core capabilities of human-centered design. The future of the designer looked bright—and strategic. That is, until it didn't.

The history of modern digital technology is ultimately a story of the power struggle between three key constituencies: software developers, business associates, and product designers. Each group's discipline is crucial to the ultimate success of an organization, but true to human nature, the balance of power is almost always unevenly distributed. The individual who holds the most power makes decisions that affect the direction of the business and its customers. The story of design's rise, fall, and rise again follows this vein.

EARLY DAYS

At the dawn of computing, software engineering teams possessed the majority of the influence. Computers—prior to the advent of the desktop personal computing revolution—were loud, large, complicated, and very expensive. User-friendly was not a term that mattered to the relatively small group of hobbyists and highly trained technologists who operated these early machines. If a monitor and keyboard were even connected to the GPU, a command prompt that accepted only specific text-based inputs was the absolutely bare-bones user interface. No point and click. No drag and drop. No problem.

In the late 1960s through the mid-1970s, research and development by trailblazers like Douglas Engelbart and Alan Kay began to influence the shift to personal computers that could potentially be used by untrained operators. Driven by Engelbart's guiding philosophy that computers could be used by all to augment human intelligence and make the world a better place, technical achievements like the computer mouse and graphical user interface (GUI) ushered in an era of user-friendly human computer interaction.

In these early days of personal computing—in order to reach the widest possible audience—design and usability were the strategy, and did that strategy ever pay off. The desktop metaphor, first introduced by Kay at Xerox Palo Alto Research Center, was designed expressly to make it easier for users to interact with their computers. The metaphor incorporated traditional office objects (files, folders, trash can, windows) into icons and a visual system that became second nature to modern computer users. This metaphor was popularized by the first Apple Macintosh in 1984 and became a worldwide phenomenon and standard bearer for GUI operating system design after the launch of Microsoft Windows 95. This user-centric strategy spawned the world's most successful and valuable companies and led to an industry that's currently worth $5 trillion globally.

In the 1990s, when we still went to physical stores and purchased software that was sold in boxes with floppy discs and CD-ROMs inside, a lot of the design work was being executed by software engineering teams. And many of the product decisions were driven by roadmaps that were owned by business teams. Although desktop computers had reached a point of maturity where they had become fairly easy for most users to operate, many of the software products being developed at the time became overly specialized and complex—forgoing the founding principles of user-centered design.

DEMOCRATIZATION

Cue the AOL 56k dial-up connection. As the World Wide Web grew exponentially from message boards and under-construction animated GIFs to an imperative for every legitimate (and illegitimate) business, graphic designers looking to get in on the digital action swapped QuarkXPress, dpi, and CMYK for FTP, pixels, and hex codes. They christened themselves "web designers." The early job responsibilities spanned branding, visual design, ad banners, graphics, interactive CD-ROMs, and respective HTML implementations. The beauty of the early Internet was how easy it was for virtually anyone to build and launch their own websites. The web democratized digital technology and design.

As Robert Kennedy, Jr. and many others have pointed out, "Democracy is messy." Not surprisingly, most early web designers approached the digital page with the same editorial lens as a paper page, trying to lay out a magazine-like grid to structure the information and control the presentation flow. But this age-old, commonsense approach would prove rather incompatible with the fluid nature of this new digital medium and the inadequate capabilities of web browsers at the time. The early web became saturated with spacer GIFs, HTML tables, pop-ups, Flash preloading screens, and dark UI patterns that sacrificed accessibility and usability.

As the web matured through the dotcom boom of the late '90s and early 2000s, so did the practice and skills of web designers. Businesses that operated on the web needed to engender trust with users, many of whom were skeptical about entering their credit card information into a form on a web page. Business owners realized website designs that were aesthetically pleasing, professional, and usable instilled more confidence in their users, encouraging them to make a purchase.

In a recent retrospective article titled "A 100-Year View of User Experience," published by the Nielsen Norman Group[1], author Jakob Nielsen explains why the web platform boom motivated executives to invest in design. Nielsen points out that with traditional software, the buyer first purchases the product and then has access to the experience. On the web, the sequence is reversed. The customer experiences the product before payment—making the user experience the gatekeeper to the money. Once again, user-centric design emerged as a winning strategy for successful companies doing business online—so successful, in fact, that according to the U.S. Department of Commerce, e-commerce transactions actually surpassed brick-and-mortar retail sales in February 2019[2].

RISE UP

Unbeknownst to us mere web mortals in the mid-2000s, a seismic shift was on the horizon—Apple launched the iPhone in 2007, and subsequently the App Store in 2008. This radical innovation opened the door to any brand, in any vertical, who wanted to release a thin slice of their software offering at our fingertips. Only a few years later, Apple's 2010 launch of the iPad rocked the landscape again, by increasing the screen real estate to dimensions comfortably situated between the size of the smartphone and the classic desktop monitor. Traditional software, once weighed down by its heavy desktop anchor, could now have a portable, slimmed-down

---

1 www.nngroup.com/articles/100-years-ux/
2 https://www.cnbc.com/2019/04/02/online-shopping-officially-overtakes-brick-and-mortar-retail-for-the-first-time-ever.html

companion. Over the next decade a tsunami of touch-enabled devices crashed into the market, reshaping user expectations about how, when, and where they could interact with software. Designers and developers watched what we knew as the web quickly evolve as we faced exponential screen size fluidity and increasingly advanced browser and technical capabilities.

As technology evolved, so did the role and specialization of the web designer. Web design (and now mobile application design) was no longer just a safe haven for graphic designers looking to transition from print to digital. Websites became more complex, transforming from simple About Us, FAQ, and Contact Us forms into full-blown web applications. The data became more robust, and a wave of user-generated content, including image libraries, streaming audio and video, and social media, made everyone a creator. An alphabet soup of specialized design roles emerged, from information architects (IAs) and user interface (UI) designers, to interaction designers (IxDs), and ultimately the user experience (UX) designer. And let's not forget about the user researchers, UX developers, UX writers, and design thinkers.

GREAT EXPECTATIONS

Gone are the days of booting up a desktop computer just to run some accounting software or going online to check last night's scores. Our computers are practically always powered on and always close at hand. We don't have to "go online" anymore; we're always connected to the Internet and to one another. Software is everywhere; it's become like oxygen. It's in our hands, in our home appliances, in our cars, on our bodies.

The preponderance and diversity of software has transformed user expectations about how they interact with machines. In barely the span of our lifetime, the average user of a computer has shifted from highly trained operators and niche hobbyists to literally everybody—a realization of Douglas Engelbart's vision. User expectations about how software should look and work (the "user experience" of interacting with the software) have become increasingly demanding. Gone are the days of computers being intimidating. Billions of people throughout the world now have an intimate and personal relationship with the computer that they carry with them daily. Interactions and interfaces can no longer be complicated because they're so commonplace. Why should the programs we use at work be so frustrating when Facebook is so easy to use?

Once again, just like during the desktop computing revolution, the introduction of the World Wide Web, and the mobile era, design is the differentiator. Businesses that understand that design—not just how a product looks, but the value it delivers—is a competitive and strategic advantage have proven time after time that they will outperform and out-last their competitors. Why? Because out of the three primary contributing roles in the product development and delivery process (design, business, and technology), *design* is the capability that is principally dedicated to understanding and delighting the end user. Customers that receive value from and feel good about their interaction with a product are more likely to be repeat customers and to tell other people about their experience, which, in turn, leads to increased customer loyalty and revenue growth.

RESTORED BALANCE

Now, having just made the case for the importance of the designer and strategy rooted in design, let's clarify that we are not advocating that the design discipline should wield more power relative to our peers. Design should be an equal to technology and business. Businesses that do this will quickly see the positive results of this balancing act. But organizations that don't hold design in equal esteem—putting more emphasis on technology or business needs—will eventually see the negative results of the power imbalance. As a strategic designer, you will not only earn design a seat of power at the table but will be a force of balance.

THE PRODUCT VISION

As a designer, and reader of this book, you've most likely been preoccupied with a nagging suspicion that there's a better way forward. Prettying up difficult-to-use interfaces and churning out a bunch of forgettable features hasn't provided you or your end users with much value. You've intuitively understood—even if you couldn't find the words to express your instincts—that without an aspirational yet achievable endpoint in mind, the project is unlikely to arrive at a meaningful destination.

Unfortunately, it's become commonplace to rely on features to spark the strategy of a product. Surely many of you may have experienced a time when a client or business partner requested detailed designs to inspire their product roadmap. Fingers crossed. Even worse, at some organizations, features are the "strategy." Either way, this often means the latest and greatest tactical processes are quickly pushed full throttle to get those features delivered. How many times have you opened up Sketch and questioned, "Why are we doing this again?" No feature-level design exercise has a prayer of clarifying a product's strategic plan.

> **Vision without action is a daydream. Action without vision is a nightmare.** — COMMONLY CLAIMED AS A JAPANESE PROVERB

A "vision" isn't just a visual exercise for the marketing department or a fun break from your day job. As the keystone of any product or service, the job of a product vision is to explain a strategy's complex connections and express the product's future intended destination. This can be done by telling the story of an experience and conceptually illustrating the offering's intentions, without getting into detailed designing. Ultimately, our product vision conveys the story of how our product or service will forge an idealized partnership between the company and their customer.

Think of it as the overarching game plan that fuses a bold future with thoughtful strategy and clearly reflects the values of an organization. Inspiring a product team to achieve greatness. It's all about ingenuity, creativity, and eventually, the smart approach to iteratively execute.

Startups get this, as do a handful of business elite—think Apple, Tesla, and Amazon. But most established businesses, don't recognize the necessity of product vision. Product vision work is shoved into a half-day effort, the kickoff of a new project. Relegated to a singular, inaugural blue-sky exercise—no more than wishful ideation. So, where's the disconnect?

Here's what's happening: the development of and adherence to a product vision is a common casualty of the transition that occurs when businesses grow from lean startups into larger, more mature enterprises. Lucky for larger businesses, designers are ready to step in and help: first, by leading a team in a new approach to create a product vision: Part II, "The Vision"; then by working with product programs to develop and align teams that execute the product vision: Part III, "Visioneering."

MAKING AN AIRTIGHT CASE

The loss of product vision is the root cause of a whole lotta enterprise problems. We strategic designers can see it oh, so clearly now. But it may not be so plainly obvious to the business. If it were, this book wouldn't need to be written. So, the designer will have to lay out a strong case to drive home the point that needs to be made. Fortunately, hindsight is an excellent tool to use to do that.

Hindsight is 20/20

Product vision is—most often—a casualty to the transitional phase where a business grows out of a lean startup and into that of a larger company. At the startup level, product vision is the ultimate necessity that both secures funding and gets an inaugural product out of the gate. Bold vision, check.

Solid strategy, check. Notably, at this stage, the product's vision and respective strategy are closely intertwined—if not, one and the same—with the fledgling company's mission. Their raison d'être.

Startups that succeed don't remain startups. A successful startup matures to a self-sustaining enterprise. And in many cases, that original product vision becomes harder to hold onto. As priorities shift, additional employees and teams are brought in to establish new initiatives, and that once clear and compelling vision becomes cloudy or fades completely. The company mission detaches from the singular product to make room for additional offerings. The strategic game plan is replaced with a tactical roadmap—a timeline that plans out feature-level deliverables. What follows is a punishing product cycle.

The once lean startup that ran like a well-oiled machine now struggles to keep in step with the nimbler way of working. The larger company tries to hold on to some semblance of an agile delivery model. But weighed down by corporate hierarchy and a lack of empowerment, the Waterfall-model habits start to slowly seep in. Desperate to keep up with small releases that can be launched in real time, a shortsightedness confines planning to the immediate near term. The focus on being accountable to the current roadmap and backlog—Scrum ceremonies, stories, and sprints—steals attention from why the work matters in the first place. Without that vision of the future, the work isn't tethered to any kind of strategic direction aimed at reaching bigger goals.

The conclusion? Product vision is often a casualty of a company's sizable growth. Yet it shouldn't be. The exceptions to the rule: the rare mega company that never lost sight of their product/service's product vision: Apple, Amazon, Google, Disney. Those company's founders mastered the art of establishing a strong vision and strategically carrying that vision thread through the entirety of a product's life. Visionary founders whose companies value design as a core competency. Coincidence? Definitely not.

RIPPLE EFFECTS

Losing product vision isn't just detrimental to the success of the respective product. Effects can polarize how a company arranges itself to work.

In many cases, from a bird's-eye view, product designers working on user experience teams are detached from the forward-thinking, innovative efforts of skunkworks or blue-sky teams. Positioned at one end, designers are dedicated to the tactical designed deliverables and usability enhancements that will launch in the near term. Within the product teams lives the user and respective experience. In contrast, at the other end are the skunkworks programs and blue-sky teams. These innovation groups focus on "visions" that push the furthest boundaries—typically in semi-secrecy with an open-ended time line. The output is rarely expected to deliver immediate commercial value. This dysfunctional, polarized setup positions the experience in the weeds and the company's future stuck in the stratosphere, leaving a vast space in the middle that should be filled with strategy-led product vision (**Figure 1.1**).

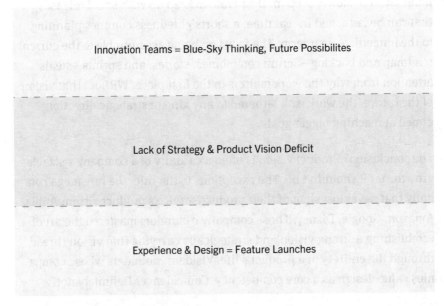

Innovation Teams = Blue-Sky Thinking, Future Possibilites

Lack of Strategy & Product Vision Deficit

Experience & Design = Feature Launches

FIGURE 1.1 Dysfunctional polarized setup.

Now with strategy-led product vision back in the fold, a business's organizational structure can rearrange and unify to reflect a comprehensive product continuum. This unification looks like design, engineering, and business comprehensively integrating to mindfully craft the best *experience* for the user. Going forward, experience is the highest guiding tenet. We are witnessing the beginning of the designer leading the charge to restore balance (**Figure 1.2**). More on this in Part II, "The Vision."

Suffice to say, the case to help non-startup businesses resurrect product vision should be airtight. But if stakeholders still aren't so easily convinced, do a thorough retrospective and illustrate how the company's growth maps to that of their flagship product. Highlight the product's lifetime milestones and how progress, or lack thereof, correlates to the absence of a clear future and lack of strategy. If that still doesn't hit home with stakeholders, then pack your designer bags; it's time to find a new business to help.

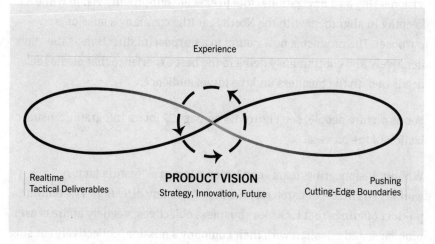

Experience

Realtime
Tactical Deliverables

PRODUCT VISION
Strategy, Innovation, Future

Pushing
Cutting-Edge Boundaries

FIGURE 1.2 Product vision unites all the pieces of the puzzle.

ENTER VISIONEERING

Here's where it all comes together. The strategic designer leads with a new approach that resurrects the practice of developing and aligning teams to the achievement of a product vision: *Visioneering*.

When the team is ready to translate all of that innovative thinking from the product vision into tangible output, how exactly do they do that? It's fair to say that this is where most product development programs get tripped up because programs are working solely against a product roadmap (or simply a laundry list of features).

Today, every product or service journey is an uncharted expedition. Now more than ever the landscape is unpredictable—quick to change due to the fast-paced nature of technology and ever-rising bar of user expectation. What the team sees in front of them now may soon shift, rendering product roadmaps obsolete. To help us maneuver this terrain, we can use Visioneering as a navigational tool to execute our product vision while keeping in alignment with the North Star (the company's mission and purpose). The product is now bound to a purposeful direction as the team iteratively and continuously delivers the best experience that meets the needs of both the business and the target audience.

For us picture people, see **Figure 1.3** on page 22 for an infographic visualization of the process.

Without Visioneering, teams can become lost in a "feature factory," working in circles, or carelessly heading off in any direction. The output: product offerings that lack clear business objectives, vaguely address user problems, and misalign with their company's mission, collectively causing a company's product ecosystem to expand in disarray and rendering an experience that's missing the mark and completely disjointed. These are very real problems that are directly related to the absence of planning for a product's product vision and the right approach to execute it. Seems pretty obvious now, right?

READY. SET. GO!

You will know if you're right for product vision work and Visioneering if you're an explorer. And most important, that thirst for exploratory adventure is driven by the hunt for the right problems to solve. Here's a mile-high view of how it works and what every vision and Visioneering-bound designer needs to learn: how to level up to become a strategic designer, the vision essentials, and expedition process and principles.

PRE-VISION

In the remaining chapters in Part I, "The Calling," you will learn step-by-step how to transform from a tactical designer to a strategic designer. As a strategic designer, you must master a handful of vehicles to have command over vision endeavors. Among those skills are great communication, a holistic understanding of the product team, and a mastering of first principles thinking.

THE VISION ESSENTIALS

Once you're christened as a fully-fledged strategic designer, it's time to lead a product vision effort! In Part II, you will have to secure dedicated resources, funding, and the privilege to operate on trust, taking the traditional business stakeholder outside their comfort zone. The product vision process spans four phases: team setup, strategy, the experience story, and production. You will learn the key attributes of the product vision team and what to expect from each role, as well as the interworking dynamics at various stages. You will learn how the team systematically explores, experiments, and refines a vision. First, by clearly articulating a strategy with a robust format that connects all of the strategic dots, you will use the power of a well-told story to help your team express the high-level intentions of a product vision without getting into specific solutions or detailed designs. You will learn a storytelling formula, step-by-step, that you can use to craft an experience story. Finally, you will learn how to produce your product vision deliverable by way of various presentation types.

VISIONEERING VISUALIZED

Setting your compass to the North Star

Strategy-led Product Vision

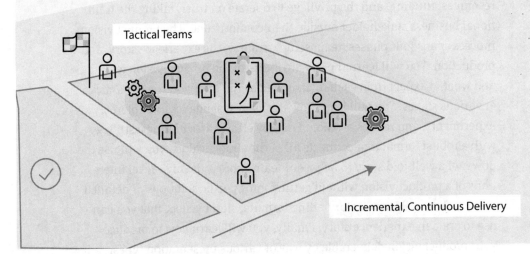

Tactical Teams

Incremental, Continuous Delivery

FIGURE 1.3 An infographic visualization of Visioneering.

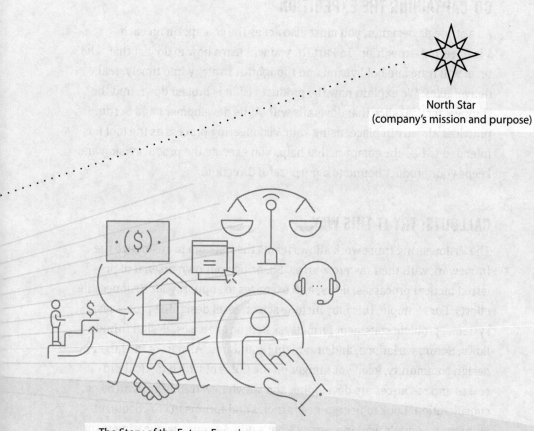

North Star
(company's mission and purpose)

The Story of the Future Experience

CO-CAPTAINING THE EXPEDITION

As a strategic designer, you must also act as the co-captain on each Visioneering expedition. In Part III, you will learn how to do just that. The team will translate bold vision and thoughtful strategy into timely, real deliverables. We explain how the product vision is broken down into the thinnest tactical slice that dovetails with Agile development and Scrum practices already in place, using your Visioneering process as the tool it is intended to be—the compass that helps you execute the product vision and keeps your product bound to a purposeful direction.

CALLOUTS: TRY IT THIS WAY

The Visioneering framework allows teams the freedom to customize the framework with their own resources. So, bring your own arsenal of preferred tactical processes, flows, and exercises to support your Visioneering efforts. For example, this may include screen-level designing processes, systems, problem statement formats, sketching exercises, design thinking flows, Scrum variations, and organizing standards. As part of the larger design community, keep your finger on the pulse of which tactical processes and resources are developing and which new trends are worthy of consideration. Look to peer-to-peer articles and forums to crowdsource opinions on what's working versus what's not. As your Visioneering team matures, so will your arsenal. What will develop is a truly mindful, flexible, and collaborative way of approaching the ask.

➡ TRY IT THIS WAY

Throughout the book, you'll see examples in "Try It This Way" features with recommendations of specific ways that have worked for us.

#INFLUENCER

It's all about ingenuity, creativity, and the smart approach to iteratively execute. As a strategic designer, one who harnesses the power of product vision and who has the ability to successfully execute that vision, you will be highly sought after. Three salaried employment options will be vying for your attention: agency life, the startup game, or working within an established business.

Of course, an agency is the fun employer with long hours, insane deadlines, and many perks. But know that most agency engagements allow for limited access to the client company. So, unless the agency is a top think tank in the product space, you won't be permitted to really dive into the business's well-guarded strategy documentation or research archives.

Then there's the startup—which might seem the obvious choice. A funded startup guarantees that the inaugural product has a viable product vision. By way of Visioneering, you settle in to nurture the product vision and act as its protector during phases of company growth. If you've landed that gig, good for you! We won't talk you out of it.

Given that solid, reputable startups aren't on every street corner and the run-of-the-mill agency work won't be fulfilling, consider employment at the sizable business. Likely that company's post-startup success has led to the business struggling with aforementioned issues that strategy-led product vision could address. Yes, it's no secret we designers have developed a like/hate relationship with the enterprise. In exchange for a steady paycheck, a 401k, and reasonable hours (which we like), we commit to a daily grind of tortuous monotony, broken promises, and professional suffering (which we hate). With every day comes a smorgasbord of surface-level obstacles to hurdle: excessive red tape, catty internal politics, and swarms of naysayers. The corporate life has not been the obvious choice for those possessing creativity. Certainly, the endless uphill battle never ceases to remind us that business has yet to fully bring design into the fold as a core capability. But as practitioners of modern-era design, our higher calling includes effecting change for the better. And the businesses of the world have plentiful cash, resources, and the brand reach to make a massive impact. And doing good is just good business. The profits will reflect that. So, if you can elevate yourself to influence high-level enterprise decisions, the possibilities are limitless. To do this, you are best positioned within the walls of large companies, rather than on the outside as a fleeting freelancer.

Once inside, how do you achieve this elevated influencer status? You know where we're going with this: it's all about product vision and a smart approach to execute it. Business is desperately in need of this kind of help. And we strategic designers are ready to help. By way of the product vision and Visioneering, you have the means to not only course-correct the wayward business ship, but also ultimately influence its direction—positioning you to lead today's slated projects and shape tomorrow's bigger picture.

The conclusion? Strategic designers and the sizable business are fated to move into a balanced partnership founded on mutually assured success. And you guessed it: that fateful time is now.

INTERVIEWS: DESIGNING FROM INSIDE THE BOX

To help you see yourself succeeding in this role, look throughout the book for "Designing from Inside the Box" features. These are interviews with industry design pros who are walking the walk and talking the talk about how they express product vision and strategy in their practice, to find success in established business.

TAKING THE LEAP

On record again, this won't be easy. You will be leaving behind the cozy comforts of the pixels and venturing into the unknown. But the first step in a journey of change is more of a leap—a leap of faith. Joseph Campbell, American author of *The Hero's Journey*, reminds us that prior to any big journey, the hero has to first hear the call to adventure, recognizing that there's something more out there[3]. Again, here's ours:

> Practitioners of modern-era design are called upon to be skilled in defining not only form and function, but *strategy*. Designers adept at modern-era design leverage their highly creative lenses to assemble connections via skillful problem solving. With this new platform, designers can envision and create the future—a gift that bears a weighty responsibility. We must use this gift to its fullest extent and effect change only for the *better*.

If you're not inspired to action yet, then this is the tough love part: are you waiting for an invitation? Stop expecting that cool project to fall in your lap as a reward for slaving over a week's worth of red-line spec'ing. Stop asking permission to do your best work. Stop asking permission to improve on the task ahead—or waiting for that quarterly review where a nondesigner will dictate how to improve your career. Aren't you tired of all the excuses? Channel your inner Nike ad and Just Do It. It's time.

---

3 *Joseph Campbell, The Hero's Journey: Joseph Campbell on His Life and Work* (Novato, CA: New World Library, 2014).

CHAPTER 2
RE-DESIGN SCHOOL

In this chapter, you will learn the techniques and practices that you can apply to level up from a *tactical designer* to a *strategic designer*. They include honing communication skills, gaining a holistic understanding of the product space, proficiency in analytics, using diplomacy, and creating persuasive documentation to connect the dots. Key to your success and influence will be the partnerships with your internal business and technology partners you are able to develop and nurture. Finally, one role you will need to embrace as a strategic leader is that of workshop facilitator. It sounds like a lot (and it is) but don't worry, you'll find step-by-step guidance in this chapter.

A DUAL ROLE FOR STRATEGIC DESIGNERS

As you transition into the strategic designer role, be sure not to lose that Sketch or Adobe Cloud license! As a strategic designer, you can expect to wear both hats: strategic designer and tactical designer—especially during your transition from tactical to strategic. Then as a fully-fledged strategic designer, your Visioneering role will ask you to "walk the walk" by occasionally producing some hands-on design documentation such as user flows, wireframes, prototypes, and user interface designs. This is critical at the start of every Visioneering effort to help the delivery process find solid footing. At that stage, you, as the strategic designer, will work closely with tactical designers on individual product teams to create the first design deliverables. Thereafter, you will step in to support the tactical team as needed. Because who better than the designer who actually *molded* the product vision, to assist translating all that innovative thinking into tangible output? Leading the tactical work by example is a great way to build credibility with your team and ensure that the product vision is being executed faithfully from the start.

In the meantime, put those wireframes on the back burner. There's a lot to unpack, so take a seat—school is in session.

A NOTE FROM THE BUTTERFLY

A quick note about strategic maturity. The pervasive delusion—really across any profession—is that with experience one's strategic chops will magically appear one day. Crossing the threshold of a decade-plus career experience does not gift a fully vested strategic mindset. The tactical designer has to be particularly careful of this falsehood.

Mind you this: if you are a designer who wants more out of your career than tactical work, *you* are the only one who can make that happen. It is your responsibility to actively realize, pursue, and achieve strategic growth. You must stay present in every moment of your metamorphosis. Step by step, you'll move your role from the end of the project funnel (output) to the beginning of the funnel, where *strategy* informs the output. These butterfly wings will be hard-earned.

But here's the cool thing about butterflies: the struggle the butterfly undertakes to break free of its cocoon determines the strength of that butterfly.

The more it struggles, the stronger its wings become. The stronger the wings, the farther the butterfly is able to fly. No doubt, these strategic designer wings will carry us the distance.

TRANSFORMING INTO THE STRATEGIC DESIGNER

Evolving from being primarily tactical (when design is focused on execution and output) to be skillfully strategic is hard work—a pilgrimage of sorts. As the transformation plays out, the tactical designer

- Cultivates communication skills beyond visual to excel in verbal and written communication

- Understands how the three main disciplines of the product team—business, design, and engineering—comprehensively work and fit together as partners.

- Hones leadership savvy by way of creative diplomacy and mastering the art of influence

- Makes decisions and proves success by referring to analytics and metrics

- Connects the dots to see what really matters and identify what may be missing

Over the course of a few years, these five turning points will collectively develop the designer's strategic maturity. Yes, that's right—this transformation will take years! You shouldn't plan on this happening overnight. You'll know that your rite of passage to strategic designer is complete when you find more success as a head coach over that of the player on the field. You earn this maturity through extensive, gritty experience.

Let's dig into each turning point.

COMMUNICATION

Exceptional communication—how we consume and share information—is a core talent of the strategic designer and crucial to product vision and Visioneering endeavors. But let's face it; many of us are introverted by nature—that's one of the reasons we may have been drawn to the design profession in the first place. Many of us tend to be more comfortable with headphones on, working independently to perfect color palettes, typography, and layouts. Evangelizing a product vision in front of a roomful of intimidating corporate executives would knock most of us way outside our comfort zone. In order to level up and become recognized as a strategic designer, you have to work to change this.

Unfortunately, communication is a skill in the designer's toolbox that isn't developed uniformly. Of the three main types of workplace communication—written, verbal, and visual—our higher education mainly focuses on visual. Visual communication is cultivated as the designer's superpower at the expense of verbal and written, which can become our kryptonite. The goal now is to elevate written and verbal communication skills to the same level as visual (**Figure 2.1**).

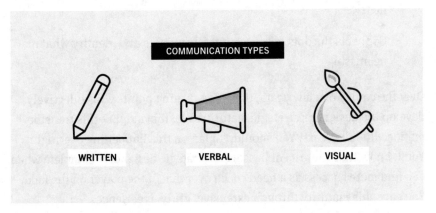

FIGURE 2.1 Become adept at all three forms of communication, not just one or two.

Each type of communication plays an important role among the operational order of how product vision unfolds:

1. Up-front, *written* communication clearly defines tasks at hand, who's responsible, and the reasons we're doing them.

2. *Visual* communication helps to sell the idea. A picture is still worth a thousand words, after all.

3. Then *verbal* communication facilitates moving the team forward.

Intertwining all three communication types will help you stream your creativity through a structured thought process.

Many designers admit that they have a difficult time expressing themselves with words. Like it or not, the way you communicate (even on Slack) isn't just a reflection of your ability to communicate; it's a reflection of your professionalism. To be taken seriously as a designer, you must be able to write and speak to your peers and stakeholders effectively. Fortunately, written and verbal communication is just like any other skill: it can improve with coaching and practice. Let's look at some practical methods you can use to improve your communication proficiency.

Improve routine writing

Start writing better emails (or texts, or design documentation, or Slack messages). How many times have you quickly written and sent a message to a colleague without giving it a second thought? If you find that you often have to clarify written messages you've sent, there's likely an opportunity for you to do better with written communication. First and foremost, slow down! Before you even start typing, make sure you take time to plan the most important point (or points) of the message you're about to send. Once you've written your first draft, reread it. Does it make sense? Does it contain any obvious grammatical errors? Any confusing or unnecessary language that detracts from your point? Are the points you were trying to make expressed simply and clearly? To put it in design terms, ask yourself, is it "clean"? We know clean means the core message is clearly surfaced and no clutter is getting in the way. For more important messages, ask your colleagues to review the content and provide feedback before hitting Send. The more you practice writing these types of internal communications, the more you'll improve.

Once you've improved your written communication among your peers, it's time to share your writing with the public. There's no shortage of free blogging platforms that allow you to post your written thoughts online. Before diving into long-form articles, try engaging in conversation by posting comments and questions on posts you've read. Twitter is another platform that allows members to post concise thoughts and engage in short bursts of written conversations with one another. Once your confidence level increases, take to platforms like your own blog/website, Medium or LinkedIn to write longer form content. Pick a topic that you're excited about (any topic—it doesn't have to be design related) and start writing. Again, plan your main points, reread your writing, and share it with your friends, family, or peers before publishing. It doesn't have to be perfect. At this stage try not to get too focused on how many people are reading, following, liking, and sharing your content. You're practicing and improving your ability to communicate via the written word for yourself first and foremost.

Write internal documentation

Another way to improve your writing skills as they pertain to your design work is to document the design principles of your organization, product, feature, or design system. These written principles act as a framework that help designers make consistent decisions about how to execute interaction and user interface designs. They are the guidelines that ensure design work is meeting the team's standards and ultimately benefiting the end user. Good design principles are clear, concise, and most important, actionable. Writing good ones will be challenging at first, but it will be excellent practice for improving your written communication skills.

Embrace analogies

An additional communication technique that can jumpstart your transition from tactical to strategic designer is the use of analogies to communicate concepts that may be challenging for people to grasp. An analogy is simply the comparison of two seemingly unlike things based on conceptually similar attributes. Analogies can make confusing or foreign topics more relatable. You'll encounter many in this book; for instance, the idea of using a compass versus a roadmap to navigate toward a product vision. A good analogy is powerful. It's done frequently when founders are describing their new startups—for example, the Airbnb of pet supplies, or the Uber of homework. We'll do more with analogies during the strategy phase of the product vision process. It's an effective way to turn an abstract concept into something tangible and even inspirational, and it's a solid approach for succinctly communicating the unique value proposition of an offering.

Speak in front of groups

The fear of public speaking, or glossophobia, is often listed as number one on any list of human phobias or social anxiety disorders. Sadly, this book can't offer a cure to help you overcome this phobia, but we can provide you with some methods for getting better at your verbal presentation skills. The easiest way to begin practicing and improving your verbal communication skills is presenting your own design work in front of your teammates. If just the thought of presenting in front of a group of people makes you want to run home and hide under the covers, start small. Grab a trusted friend or colleague and present your latest design work to them one on one. Describe the user for whom you created the design and the problem that you're attempting to solve. Talk through your design decisions. Make sure that you're able to speak to the intentions behind each decision. Most important, invite questions and feedback to spark a dialog. This will help you think and speak without a prepared script. As you gain confidence speaking to one person, do the same with incrementally larger groups. Find safe environments where you can present to your design peers, and gradually work your way up to presenting in front of larger, less familiar groups of people. Once you've gained enough confidence, start submitting proposals to speak at local meetups and design events. Just keep practicing!

If you've successfully shaken off your nerves and you're more comfortable standing in front of a group to share your design work or deliver a verbal presentation, consider seeking out classes in improvisation to strengthen your presentation technique. Improv classes aren't all about turning you into the next Amy Poehler or Chris Farley (although that would certainly make design reviews much more entertaining). The classes will improve your ability to remain comfortable and confident while standing up in front of a room full of people and thinking on your feet. Let's face it—how many times have you witnessed a speaker awkwardly having to fill time while the facilities team figures out how to plug a MacBook into their AV system. Improvisation classes also teach students how to be better listeners and observers of human behavior, how to be fully present in the moment, and how to collaborate with others on the fly—all skills that will make you a better designer. Looking for a perfect idea for a teambuilding activity? Several groups offer improv classes to businesses. Or, if you can't get your company to pay for it, every major city has improv troupes that offer classes and workshops for beginners.

Don't forget to listen

Lastly, the other side of good communication is effective listening. In the workplace, most conversations are working toward an agreement. Try this going forward: at the end of your next work-related conversation, summarize what you've heard into high-level points and actionable takeaways. This concise soundbite helps keep all parties on the same page, sets expectations, and keeps everyone moving toward optimal efficiency.

DEVELOP A HOLISTIC UNDERSTANDING OF THE PRODUCT TEAM

Foster a shift in product team collaboration, embracing a more human-centric mindset—with you, the strategic designer, emerging as a capable force. This shift is what triggers the internal product players to rearrange and unify. This unification will look like the three main disciplines of the product team—design, engineering, and business—integrating to mindfully craft the best possible experience for the user (**Figure 2.2**).

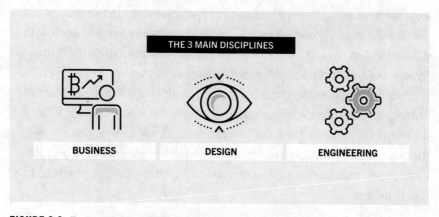

FIGURE 2.2 Foster partnerships among the key disciplines.

Members of each discipline will have their role to play but this time around as truly interdependent partners. Gone are the days where the disciplines all played semi-nicely but were ultimately separate entities. This integration lifts the practice of user experience out from the usability weeds and restores it as the larger overarching umbrella founding father Don Norman intended. Experience is now the highest guiding tenet among all three main disciplines. This is the new, revitalized product team—rooted in true partnership and collaboration.

As a strategic designer, you have developed a holistic understanding of how the product team's main disciplines—business, design, and engineering—comprehensively work and fit together. This does not mean the designer should become a one-stop shop—acting in all three capacities as designer, developer, and product owner. You expertly understand the various aspects of design and how design fits into the product team but at the same time are well versed *beyond* just design to have a solid working knowledge of business and engineering. You understand the key attributes of each role and how the roles interplay at various stages of both a product vision effort and respective Visioneering endeavor (more on this in part two and part three of the book). Imagine yourself as an orchestra conductor; a conductor is not necessarily able to play each instrument but is at least familiar with the capabilities of every instrument in the orchestra. You should expertly orchestrate the team to optimally execute against the product vision. You will see the bigger picture and anticipate the butterfly effect of any contribution—how one feature ripples across the overall product and impacts the experience. Here, your leadership responsibilities are to 1) inspire incredible work, and 2) be accountable to making sure decisions are made to move the ball forward. Although you may not be the one making the decision, you facilitate the decision-making process by applying pressure on the party who *is* making the decision to do so in a timely manner.

As discussed in Chapter 1, "The State of the Designer," the step up to elevated tactical designer involves becoming very comfortable with technology—so much so that this designer is the bridge that connects design to engineering (and if that doesn't describe you, that may be the best place to start, before embarking on the strategic designer journey).

With design and engineering down, you have one final discipline to tackle: business. Your challenge, should you accept it, is to emerge as the bridge that connects design to business. Recognizing the importance of a close business partner alliance, you work to narrow the gap—tearing down the barriers that create rifts between creatives and business folk. You can accomplish this goal, in part, by recognizing that designers and business partners need to learn how to speak the same language. That means you have to care enough to overcome any lack of business literacy to learn to speak the language of business— competently.

The topics of business and business economics are dense and complex, and they come with a steep learning curve. Thankfully, becoming well rounded with product-related business acumen does not mean you are setting out to earn an MBA. You can—don't let us stop you—but certainly do not need to. The strategic designer can keep it simple by sticking to the fundamental concepts that directly relate to finding success with product vision. The fundamental concepts you have to learn include industry, competition, market, demand, goals and objectives, brand, and last but not least, internal operations. You should be clear on each concept, how each concept relates to another, and how it plays into your product vision. Chapter 5, "Strategy: Connecting the Dots," focuses on helping you become better acquainted with these fundamental concepts. You should become comfortable with these topics, but ultimately, you know your strength. Your task going forward: become involved with business kick-offs, status updates, and the occasional working session. You can lean on your super smart business partners to do the heavy lifting.

As you work to become fluent in the basics of business, it's worth mentioning where the designer's business illiteracy problem stems from: a shortsightedness in our formal higher education. University design curricula focus on learning the artistic and digital craft, with a focus on tactical skills. But once you graduate college, you may find it difficult to make the leap to understanding how design fits into the businesses you want to work for. You likely haven't acquired much—if any—business acumen through your schooling. This fact makes it difficult to see how your product design work fits into the complex nature of a company's operation. Hence, while pixel savvy, you may be business illiterate.

This lack of business know-how persists in your design career. It becomes a hard-to-pinpoint obstacle that keeps you at a continual disadvantage, with real-world implications. Corporations primarily structure the company's hierarchical ladders, promotions, and raises around those disciplines that deliver the most perceived value—traditional business roles and engineering roles. If your role falls into the "other" category—which designing often does—you're at the bottom of an often confusing and limiting career ladder—as is your compensation. So, whether or not money and upward mobility is a motivator, know that a firm grasp of business proficiency is a must to successfully practice as a strategic designer.

Trust that developing business sensibility will take a determined effort and is within your abilities. Start by recruiting tutors. Your colleagues went through years of schooling—with both undergraduate and graduate degrees to prove it, making your workplace the perfect place for a make-shift business school! Expert business strategists, experienced analysts, and market researchers are all within arm's reach. Reach across the aisle and ask these friends for help learning the language of business. Humility is always a good place to start . . . well, first buy them a latte, then ask for help. Ask if you can sit in on some of their meetings. Regular exposure to everyday business terminology will help you grasp the ABCs of business basics. With practice, you will develop an ear for identifying contextual takeaways. You will be able to evaluate and execute business needs with practical design application. Picture this, in the not-too-far future: you're presenting to stakeholders, walking them through a crystal-clear case of how you anchored design decisions with business objectives top of mind. Priceless.

CREATIVE DIPLOMACY

A stellar product vision and a smart approach to execute it isn't enough to guarantee a product's success. Any established business is loaded with political landmines, tense rivalries, and excessive red tape. This is where diplomacy comes in. A state diplomat's job is to help parties find common ground peacefully despite varying—or drastically opposing—opinions. As a strategic designer, you are a creative diplomat. You must work behind the scenes to nurture relationships and facilitate collaboration among the three product disciplines (design, business, and engineering) to protect the interests of the user. As a creative diplomat, you are always negoti-ating on behalf of the user and reminding politically motivated internal stakeholders that their customers' needs are paramount. Designers who are able to bring everyone to the table can direct the conversation and, ultimately, the outcome.

 DESIGNING FROM INSIDE THE BOX INTERVIEW

For the designer working inside the enterprise, what skill is the key to finding success as a leader?

To find success as a leader, the strategic designer needs to be a "trusted" expert. That trust is earned through creative diplomacy. Creative diplomacy is the ability to frame the problem in the language of each party that makes it abundantly clear the solution was created with their needs in mind. Creative diplomacy is assumed to be "design by committee." This is wrong. It does not mean that you compromise the design to the lowest common denominator of acceptance, nor lose your ability to offer meaningful critique by walking on eggshells. Creative diplomacy is the strategic designer's ability to read a room. This means a strategic designer not only understands the customer's problem to solve but truly understands the business objectives, the culture they operate in, and the motivations of those partners they are working with to solve the problem. Then it is on the designer to always be demonstrating the creative path you are all taking is achieving every party's interests.

— CHRIS WHITLOCK, FOUNDER, CREATIVE DIRECTOR
CHANGEUPIGLOBAL LLC

The key to diplomacy is building trust among all parties. The more trust you're able to build, the easier it will be for you to influence the politics swirling around you. Trust is built by building relationships. If you eat lunch solely with other designers or alone at your desk every day, you're not building much trust. If you're participating only in meetings attended primarily by designers, you're not building trust beyond your design peers. To make the transition to a strategic designer, you have to build relationships with people outside of the design department. Offer to buy the front-end developer on your team a coffee. Sit down at the lunch table with business analysts and product owners. Schedule one-on-ones with the stakeholders who are involved in making important decisions about the products and business. You're going to have to get out of your comfort zone. Get to know these people and what matters to them professionally and personally. Share information about yourself and your vision of how a focus on design and your customers can benefit the business. Trust doesn't happen overnight. It's hard to earn and easy to lose. Building relationships is the first step toward establishing the rapport that will enable your creative diplomacy.

Creative diplomacy is the backbone of design leadership. The thoughtful diplomatic design leader is a trusted adviser, confidante, and clever negotiator. Creative diplomacy allows you to build productive relationships. Take the time to build rapport with your product partners and develop those relationships. Be a great listener. Do a favor for your partners when you can. Check in with partners after meetings, inquiring about their views and opinions. Know the value of setting a good example and show your team how to act in accordance with respectable core values. Be commanding, not demanding.

BY THE NUMBERS—ANALYTICS, METRICS AND MONEY

For many of us, numbers can be scary, intimidating, or—let's be frank—just boring. But as a strategic designer you have to be able to refer to analytics and metrics to prove Visioneering success. At the end of the day, success must be measurable to matter. We measure success by how well we solved a problem for the user through the lens of business objectives. Analytics is how we do this. When you gather information on human behavior, the results provide insights into the effectiveness of your solutions against the strategy. You may not be the analytic and metric owner—Visioneering has dedicated a core role to this expertise. But you do have to participate in brainstorming measurement plans and understanding insights. And you must grasp how those insights translate into takeaways that will inform design decisions.

Here's the skinny on designers and data. Designers can be an invaluable asset to analyst, statistician, and researcher colleagues when it comes to searching for a needle in a haystack, or in our case, for an insight in a stack of data. Any tactical designer who does well with data visualizations and infographics knows this to be true. The designer's keen eye is perfect for scanning large columns of numbers to spot hard-to-find patterns.

➡ TRY THIS TRICK OF THE TRADE

First, you have to remove the burden of searching for meaning within the data. Numbers are just shapes; think of the numbers as shapes and the length of each number in terms of width. Scan the document, looking for increasing or decreasing width and keeping an eye out for sequencing shapes and repeatable combinations. Mark the areas that stand out the most and discuss the findings with your colleagues. Your visual observations have the power to improve the group's ability to make the big connections during brainstorming.

The barrier to your offering this type of help could be rooted in insecurity. We creatives can feel unworthy or not smart enough to take on the big bad world of data. But if you give yourself permission to put yourself out there, imagine the gems and connections that could unveil a path toward innovative discoveries.

A strategic designer should be able to have an intelligent conversation with business colleagues about the pros and cons of a product's business model options. During these conversations, you should set out to understand how the proposed business model—the plan to make money—will affect your team's design decisions. For example, a financial services company may have a default long-term business model for investment offerings. The customer opens an investment account, with no upfront cost. In a few years' time, the company will make money off the profitable return of that customer's investment. The better the company's brokers manage that fund, the better the customer does, and the higher the company's profit. The customer and the company are in it for the long haul. But what about that same financial services company making a move into providing financial advice? An advisory offering (such as: help me understand my money) might be better offered as one-time fee or a monthly subscription business model. In that scenario, the customer might pay a fat flat fee every month with the ability to cancel every 30 days. Your design decisions should take this into account. The team will prioritize an onboarding experience that quickly gets the user up and running and seeing value right off the bat.

THE CONNECTOR OF THE DOTS

When you're zoomed 1600 percent into your design file, all you can see are individual pixels. Looking this closely at a design can help you detect tiny details, but it's difficult to see the design in its entirety. It's impossible, as they say, to see the forest for the trees. The final step in the transition from tactical to strategic is the ability to zoom out—sometimes way, way out—from the pixel-based minutia and be able to see how a product or business fits into an entire market ecosystem. The final stretch sees the designer confidently connecting the dots—able to distinguish the dots that matter from the dots that are irrelevant.

When most of us begin our careers as product designers, we're thrilled to be able to get paid for adding value by applying the techniques we had learned and creating tactical design deliverables like user flows, wireframes, and interface designs. The skill to create clear design documentation that facilitates the product team's ability to deliver a product to their end users is critical and highly valuable. A capable designer focused on executing usable and functional interface designs is an asset to any product team. In the early stages of your career, you'll most likely be asked to design a new feature for an existing product, and you won't think to question why. You'll be excited that you've been given a challenge to solve with your design skills, never considering how this new feature may affect how users interact with other areas of the product.

As most designers gain career experience, we naturally begin seeking to understand how individual parts join together to create a whole. We begin asking questions about how each feature, each interaction, affects the broader user experience. We seek to learn more about our users and their needs. We may start pushing back by questioning whether a new feature may even be necessary. This ability to start asking meaningful questions and connecting the dots is the final turning point from tactics to strategy. So, when you start finding that you are more frequently taking a step back and seeing beyond just the pixels to an interconnected network of cause and effect, the evolution has begun. You're ready to apply everything you've learned about communication, business, diplomacy, and metrics to begin the journey to become a strategic designer.

FIND COACHES AND A MENTOR

Developing strategic maturity is challenging and will require a lot of dedicated practice—and help. Be sure and find short-term coaches and, if you can, a long-term mentor who is invested in your future success.

Begin by evaluating candidates to be your short-term coaches. Recruit a colleague who will coach you on a specific task, such as how to improve written communication with a brief or how to facilitate an upcoming workshop. Finding a coach should be fairly easy. A coaching exercise is a direct ask and a short-term commitment, so you have a good chance of that colleague agreeing. Bring a coach in at the start of an effort. Send an email with an estimate of the number of half-hour sessions you anticipate needing. To accommodate the coach's schedule, you might offer to come into work early, stay late, or have working lunches. Book all the sessions with the coach upfront to keep the exercise timeboxed and expectations crystal clear.

A mentor is the harder find. You should look for a mentor within your current organization—and be clear on your request. But do not ask an acquaintance to be your mentor right off the bat! A mentor/mentee relationship is rooted in a friendship, which takes time to develop. The mentor is investing extra time and energy into a career that's not their own, so obviously it has to be for someone they actually *like* being around. Unlike a coach, who is walking you through proper techniques and often giving you the answers that accomplishes a tangible goal, a mentor won't help you by doing the work for you. They're honest and will keep things real. They guide you to successful outcomes by way of hindsight of their own growth, encouragement, and support that motivates you to put in the hard work. Know that relationship will be hands-on for only as long as you are both working for the same employer. When either you or the mentor leaves that employer, it's on you to find a new mentor. Going forward, collect a roster of mentors you can regularly stay in touch with.

BUILDING PARTNERSHIPS

Visioneering success hinges on the strength of the product team's dynamic collaboration, especially between you, the strategic designer, and your business peers. Unfortunately, in recent years, design and business have been at odds. Every weekday, the two face off in a very real tug of war between the desires of the business and the needs of the user has developed. This tug of war has fractured the product team—business and design each taking respective sides, and the two camps have remained at odds. You will have to be the broker of peace, extending an olive branch with the better way forward: as trusted, collaborative partners. Both you and your business peers will have to transition from the mindset of individual contributors who both work in silos to that of partners, with shared responsibilities and founded on mutual respect. To get here, start by practicing empathy.

Empathy at work has been, traditionally, considered a weakness. But really, practicing empathy at work is a strength. We designers leverage compassionate empathy daily to tune into our beloved users—slipping on the user's shoes to share their feelings, reactions, and concerns. There's more than enough empathy to go around, so let some spill over onto your business peers. Just as you do with your customer, you have to step back and view the workplace from your colleagues' perspective. Exhibiting empathy doesn't mean having to agree with your business partner's position. By taking the time to tune into what they're going through and putting in the effort to figure out a way forward, you are showing your partner that you understand and care.

Here are a few ways to start applying empathy to professional partnerships:

- **Write out a partnership contract:** Start your newfound partnership on the right foot by clearly defining each individual role, shared responsibilities and the collaborative tasks. Book a monthly one-on-one meeting to check in with each other. Working together closely every day means there's no room to be inauthentic. It also means accepting each other as you are and being reasonable about expectations.

- **Adhere to the platinum rule:** In kindergarten we learned the golden rule: treat others the way that you would want to be treated. An empathetic take on the golden rule is the platinum rule: treat others the way that *they* want to be treated. That means we are regularly tuning in to understand what that treatment is.

- **Check into couples counseling:** There's a reason the colleagues you spend the most time with are referred to as work spouses. Every now and then, try this couples counseling exercise. Ask your business partner to tell you about a work-related situation. Observe their facial expressions, body language, and tone of voice to gauge what emotions they are feeling: anger, frustration, joy, excitement, etc. Write all the perceived emotions down, share the list with your business partner, and discuss. Did you correctly identify their emotions? Regular sessions like these keep the lines of communication open.

- **Activate listening skills:** Every now and then your partner will just need to be heard. That means being fully present and listening with both your ears and your heart. Be sure to tune into nonverbal communication, which is sometimes the more honest form of communication.

- **Regularly show appreciation:** Take the time to genuinely express how much you appreciate your business partner and their work. When you give praise—via a text message or email—spend the extra time to make the words memorable and specific. At the very least, use the words "I appreciate you and your hard work."

Just remember, as you take on new responsibilities, beyond the tactical, your business peers will be in a similar spot with their own growing pains. So, love your business partner and put in the effort to form a tight bond. From here on forward, you are now attached at the hip. The success of Visioneering hinges on a truly integrated partnership.

THE FINAL STEP: THE WORKSHOP FACILITATOR

Welcome to the boss level. Your official coronation as a strategic designer isn't complete until you've combined everything that you've learned and put your skills to work facilitating a workshop. Successful workshop facilitation requires a keen ability for managing group dynamics, the ability to adapt and improvise, proficiency with active listening and consensus building, and a generous helping of confidence. Just like everything else that you've read about in this chapter, it also takes practice. Full disclosure: even after facilitating dozens of workshops, you can still get nervous;

it's completely normal. Facilitation can also be exhausting. You're going to want to make sure you get a good night's sleep (or two) afterward. If you're still up for the challenge and ready to embrace the mantle of strategic design, read on for some well-worn advice on how to become a facilitation guru.

PREPARATION

The foundation of a facilitator's success is preparation. There are dozens, maybe hundreds, of memorable quotes about the advantages of planning and preparation—and for good reason. The real make-it-or-break-it moment happens long before the workshop even begins, during the planning. Your odds of conducting a productive workshop increase if you make sure that everyone involved understands what's expected of them and what you hope to get out of the workshop.

Start your workshop plan by setting up time to meet with your key teammates and stakeholders. First, determine if a workshop is really necessary. Surely many of you have received a vague email invite to a last-minute workshop, only to ask hours later: *why*? So, to avoid this, and be considerate to everyone's time, ask thoughtful questions first. Here are some examples:

- Is the team starting a brand-new project or an important phase/feature of an existing product?

- Are they addressing a customer need that hasn't been met before?

- Is the business model changing?

Workshops are most useful when it's important to gather key contributors to discuss and establish a clarity of purpose and explore potential solution ideas. If you decide that a workshop is the right next step for your team, make sure you build consensus around the objectives, attendees, and agenda for the workshop (**Figure 2.3**).

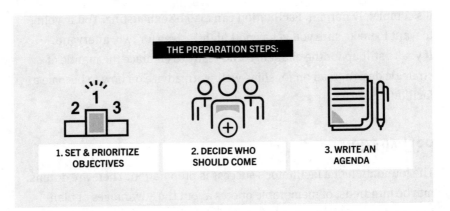

FIGURE 2.3 Don't just dive in. Be prepared.

1. Set and Prioritize Objectives: Create a prioritized list of the workshop objectives. The completion of each objective on the list is your rubric for success. The goal is to complete every objective by the end of the workshop. For instance, if the main objective of a workshop was to define the scope of an MVP and the workshop ends before accomplishing that goal, the workshop missed the mark. Once the objectives are listed, prioritized, and agreed on, it's helpful to set expectations by sharing the list beforehand with all workshop participants. On the day of, facilitators should write the list on a whiteboard or large sheet of paper so it's visible to everyone in the room. When participants feel as though they've completed an objective, strike it off the list.

2. Decide Who Should Come: Now that you know what you want the workshop to accomplish, decide who needs to attend. Attendees should include anyone who will help accomplish the agreed-on objectives. They will likely include

- All immediate team members

- Key members of product teams who may overlap with your work

- Subject matter experts (SMEs) who can provide additional insights into business and user needs, analytics, the competitive space, and so forth

- Senior stakeholders whose input may be required for approvals

- Additional innovative or creative types, who tend to ask good questions and envision creative solutions

Not everyone needs to attend for the entire duration. SMEs and senior stakeholders can often attend for 30–60 minutes to provide input and then be sent on their way. The sweet spot is anywhere from 8 to 12 active, full-time workshop participants.

3. Write an Agenda: The third and final step in the pre-workshop process is to craft an agenda. Depending on what you want to achieve, workshops can last anywhere from a couple hours to an entire workweek (we're looking at you, Google Design Sprint). Determine the actions that will need to be taken to achieve all your objectives and try your best to figure out how much time each one will take. Accurate estimation takes a lot of trial and error. As a general rule, it tends to be better to allow for more time and not need it than not to have enough. If the workshop attendees are actively engaged (which is usually the case), you'll probably feel like you have to rush through the final hour. You should also assign owners to each action on your agenda. Facilitators shouldn't be the only people standing in front of the room and presenting information. For example, assign time for your SMEs to walk through a competitive analysis. Product management can discuss key analytics. Your design researcher can review the results of the latest usability test or a heuristic analysis of your existing product. Again, in the spirit of setting clear expectations, share the agenda beforehand and give everybody enough time to prepare their material.

FACILITATION

Now that you're fully prepared, you are ready to facilitate the workshop. Facilitating workshops per a product vision is thoroughly addressed in the next section of the book. But here are some additional universal facilitation techniques that you can use during any workshop:

- Establish working agreements.

- Stay on time and keep the focus on end users.

- Push for prioritization—what matters most?

- Ask provocative questions.

- Capture assumptions, truths, and How Might We statements.

- Display and cross off workshop objectives.

Establish Working Agreements: When you're getting started with the workshop, make sure you establish working agreements for everyone who is participating. Ask all participants to offer some rules of engagement and write them down for all to see. Common workshop working agreements are

- Limit the use of phones or laptops except during breaks.

- Don't speak while others are speaking.

- Challenge assumptions.

- Be open minded.

Stay on time and keep the focus. As facilitator, in addition to keeping the group on task and on time, keep the participants focused. Most design workshops will be focused on the end user. But all too often we get wrapped up in deadlines, technology, and solutions, and forget about those for whom we're designing: our customers! Take time to make sure that all attendees understand user needs and empathize with your target audience. Walk through the customer journey or user flow to illustrate your target audience's experience. As conversations veer off to tech stacks and deadlines, try to refocus all attendees back on the value you can deliver to your end users.

Push for prioritization. Speaking of prioritization, a good facilitator helps participants prioritize what matters. This can be one of the most challenging tasks a facilitator will encounter. Many of the people we work with—especially those among the business persuasion—bristle at the thought of prioritizing. After all, everything is important! Your job is to patiently and diplomatically remind your peers that all things can't be equally important. Asking questions like "Which target audience currently matters the most to our business?," "We can get to all of this eventually, but where do we want to begin today?," or "What are the quick wins?" will help your efforts give more weight to the issues that matter.

Ask provocative questions! A workshop is an opportunity to challenge the norm and think big. Diplomatically asking "why?" and "what if?" questions can help reframe customer problems, reaffirm priorities, break down legacy thinking, and open up unexplored opportunities. Why is your competitor's product better than yours? What if you decided not to do this? Why will this matter to your users? These are just a few examples of questions that can spark innovative approaches.

Capture assumptions, truths, and How Might We statements. This last tip will help participants stay engaged and actively listening during the workshop. When the session begins, pass out sticky notes and pens to all participants. Explain to them that throughout the workshop they should write down notes on those stickies in the following categories: Assumptions, Truths, and "How Might We's?" If a participant hears something that's an assumption—it could be an assumption about your users, your competitors, success metrics—they should write the assumption on a sticky note. The same goes for things we absolutely know to be true (often derived from metrics). There are always more assumptions than truths.

The final category, "How Might We's?," is focused on capturing seeds of ideas based on the problems we're trying to solve. For instance, if it's been observed that your current user flow takes too long for your customers to complete, a "How Might We?" sticky may read, "How might we speed up the current check out process?" Every so often gather the stickies that have been written and place them in the three categories on a wall or whiteboard for all to see. Group similar topics together and review all the content with participants.

Display and cross off workshop objectives. All the while, as the group completes each workshop objective, cross it off the whiteboard list. With each strike, you are closer to success! Know, striking that last objective off the list is truly a satisfying feeling. The entire group will feel a sense of accomplishment. Be sure to follow-up with participants to get their feedback on the format of the workshop. This can be an online survey or an in person conversation. And always remember to send a thank you email.

Unfortunately, there's no guarantee that great work will come from a workshop. But regardless of the outcome, your ability to skillfully facilitate these types of workshops will carry you officially over the threshold from tactical to strategic designer.

FAIR WARNING

Out of the gate, be prepared to encounter pushback—a lot of pushback. As you make your way from tactical designer to strategic designer, you will find the personal journey of transformation challenging. Not only because self-change is difficult—altering long-held behaviors and thinking is hard stuff—but because your change will cause a domino effect to ripple across the larger product program. And that will ruffle feathers. Just whispering the word *change* in the enterprise will spook anyone within earshot. Except the designer. Designers not only have a unique mentality that embraces change, they also celebrate it. But many people (think of that long-term employee who depends on flying underneath the radar) will resist change.

Pushback will look like extra red tape, some passive-aggressive putdowns and the naysayers barraging you with their personal fear-of-failure issues. Just let it all roll off your back. You got this! That's not to say, eventually a few years in, all of that negativity will chip away at your armor to leave even the most resilient of us exhausted, depressed, and questioning your abilities (been there, done that). To circumnavigate this, be sure to form a support group with fellow designers undergoing the same transformation. There's strength in numbers. Also, this may seem contradictory, but don't underestimate the power of human connection. Take the time to explain to those meddlesome colleagues why you are pursuing this different path. Building connections, one naysayer at a time, can slowly turn the tide in your favor. And always remember, the pushback is a testament to the designer. Ruffling feathers and bearing the brunt of doing so is just part of the metamorphosis. These butterfly wings are worth it, but hard-earned.

CHAPTER 3

MASTER CLASS: FIRST PRINCIPLES THINKING

This is where you earn your black belt as a strategic designer. As designers, we understand that working through our personal creative process tends to feel something like "This is a great idea! Hang on, this is impossible. This sucks. I suck! Maybe this could work? This is awesome! But wait..." Rinse and repeat.

Some skepticism isn't necessarily a bad thing if you apply it productively. From the start to the end of the product vision process, you'll call upon two fundamental and related concepts to calm your concerns and ensure that you're formulating a product vision that's simultaneously effective and groundbreaking.

The first concept, validation, is fairly straightforward:

Validation involves consistently identifying, observing, and measuring proof points to make sure that you're on the right path to meeting the needs of both your internal business stakeholders and your target audience.

The second concept, first principles thinking, is more elusive and challenging to master:

First principles are measurable and proven truths or fundamental laws of nature.

First principles thinking involves identifying and challenging assumptions and breaking problems down into their component parts to truly understand them.

Perfecting these approaches will enable you and your team to identify and verify what your users really need and deliver the most original and cutting-edge concepts that have the potential to truly transform your users' lives, the business, and the respective industry at large.

In this chapter we'll dive into these two seemingly unrelated practices, both of which challenge the basic tendency for most of us to *mistake assumptions for facts*. Techniques that apply validation and first principles thinking to your process will give you confidence in your product vision endeavor. Like any worthwhile skill, mastering these more advanced concepts will take perseverance and patience; it may also make those around you who are pleased with the status quo very uncomfortable. In the end it will be worth the effort. Let's begin.

SHADOWS ON THE CAVE WALL

Plato, in Book VII of *The Republic*, shared his famous "Allegory of the Cave." This tale describes a group of people confined to the inside of a dark cave for their entire lives. Not only that, but their heads are directed only at the cave wall immediately in front of them upon which shadows are cast. These shadows, projected by the people, animals, and objects in the light of a fire behind them, represent the cave dwellers' only reality. This life and these shadows are all they've even known until one day, one of the prisoners is freed from the cave.

The freed prisoner is able to turn around, and after his eyes begin to adjust, see and feel the fire that was projecting the shadows on the wall. Finally, after gaining the strength to walk, he's able to leave the cave entirely to explore the world beyond. After exiting the dark cave, he's nearly blinded by the sunlight. He finds himself confused and frightened by the forms that he encounters. The colors, textures, and dimensions are far richer and more tangible than the shadows the cave dweller was accustomed to experiencing. It's difficult for the freed prisoner to accept the new forms, but eventually he realizes that the shadows on the wall were just dark, one-dimensional images of a more vivid, multisensory reality.

What does this bizarre cave story have to do with a product vision? Pause for a moment to question how you developed your understanding of the world around you. Consider the acquired "knowledge" that will lead you to decide how to design, what to design, who to design for, what problem to attempt to solve, and what ultimately will be considered successful:

- Where did your perceived understanding of the customer and their needs come from?

- How much of your information comes from firsthand, fact-based inquiry?

- How much of that information was passed along to you, filtered from second and thirdhand sources (like a game of telephone)?

Too often, those of us tasked with creating products that our end users will value are doing our work based on shadows cast on the wall. We're making important decisions based on assumptions and shared beliefs. Too often these assumptions and shared beliefs can feel so real that we accept them as truth without questioning whether there's more to the story—more than shadows cast on the wall.

WHAT ARE FIRST PRINCIPLES?

In Plato's cave allegory, first principles are represented by the forms that the freed prisoner experienced when he left the cave. These forms—material objects and living creatures that exist beyond the dimly lit confines of the cave—were the true fundamental components that produced the shadows projected on the cave wall. The shadows that the cave dweller perceived as reality, or shared beliefs, represent reasoning by analogy—knowledge based on unearned, assumed information.

First principles are not shared beliefs. They're not cliched platitudes often heard in business like "This is the way we've always done things around here" or "This is how our competition does things." Again:

First principles are measurable and proven truths or fundamental laws of nature.

First principles thinking involves identifying and challenging assumptions and breaking problems down into their component parts to truly understand them.

This way of thinking is very challenging—challenging to do it yourself and challenging to advocate to others. Succeeding with first principles thinking will require a two-pronged approach consisting of diligently focusing on and highlighting truths over assumptions and using diplomacy to bring others around to your way of truly seeing the world.

QUESTION EVERYTHING

At this level you're aware that design is so much more that "how it looks." Design is a process. It's a mindset—a way of thinking. The best designers ask the best questions. Asking great questions is at the heart of first principles reasoning. Zen Buddhists have a concept known as Shoshin (初心) or "beginner's mind." Practicing Shoshin means leaving behind your preconceived notions about a subject—even a subject that you may know very well—and being open to learning as if you were still a beginner. Asking "why?" and "what if?" is a young child's approach to learning about the world. Kids are the best learners because they have no preconceptions. They're constantly asking questions about the world around them. They haven't yet learned that asking a lot of questions is a good way to get into trouble with an impatient adult.

Let's take it back to the ancient Greeks for a specific method of questioning that will help you drill down to first principles: Socratic Questioning.

- Ask clarifying questions—What does this data actually mean?

- Ask questions that challenge assumptions—How might we validate or disprove this assumption?

- Ask questions that probe for evidence—What caused this to happen in the first place?

- Ask questions that probe alternate perspectives—What's the alternative? Who benefits from this?

- Ask questions about the consequences of your thinking—What are the ramifications of assuming this is true?

- Ask questions that challenge your original question—Why is this important?

When you and your team make observations that are indicative of possible user problems, turn to the Socratic Questioning method of asking questions to identify and challenge assumptions. It will be difficult for most at first, but like anything with practice and repetition, it will eventually come more naturally. This approach will open doors to new visionary ideas that lead you away from doing things the way you've always done them or imitating your competitors.

APPLYING FIRST PRINCIPLES: VERIFY INFORMATION

Thanks to lessons learned from Plato, we should keep in mind that, depending on how we learned about an opportunity, a user, and their problem, we can't automatically take these findings at face value. Even discoveries based on empirical data, like shadows that appear real, can be worth deeper analysis to validate their credibility and relevance to our work.

USER FEEDBACK

With an existing product or service, it's important to collect and review user feedback, keeping in mind that *the plural of anecdote isn't data*. Where possible, collect quantitative data—typically larger quantities of data that's measured and expressed numerically—about how your product is being used. Even with hard data, however, it's important to challenge assumptions and question how the information is interpreted from the standpoint of the target audience.

For instance, your business partners may value a "time spent on site" metric as proof indicating a successful product and user experience (i.e., the more time people spend interacting with the product, the more engaged and satisfied they are). But the case may be that users are frustrated that it takes too long to find the information they're looking for, and they end up deciding to leave the site without successfully completing their task. This single quantitative metric without additional context is capable only of showing how much time users spend on your website; it can't explain that, for many users, more time on the website may indicate a frustrating and negative experience.

Beyond app store ratings and reviews, some larger companies are using data analytics teams and tools to monitor customer sentiment from a variety of sources. These sources may include long-form articles and blog posts by professional journalists/reviewers and customers, ratings and reviews from a variety of retail websites, user-generated content on social media, customer service call logs, and comments submitted directly to the business via a feedback form. The data is compiled and analyzed to present user feedback trends. Machine learning can be deployed against large data sets to attempt to analyze user sentiment. However, errors can occur. For example, consider a vacuum cleaner company that is trying to determine customers' true meaning of the word "sucks."

SURVEYS

Surveys (we're seeing them all too often popping up on websites these days) are another way of collecting large amounts of user praise and criticism to spot potential problems. NPS (Net Promoter Score) has become a common (albeit controversial) single-question survey that companies use to measure user loyalty and satisfaction. Similar to qualitative analytics, the power in surveys lies in making sure the questions you ask capture the right *kinds* of information. Notably:

- Is the feedback you're collecting from users actionable?

- Does it deliver insights aligned with your product strategy?

Only then can your team confidently use the feedback to make decisions about future improvements.

With surveys it's also important to keep in mind that users willing to take the time to complete a satisfaction survey often do so in response to a negative experience. Though still extremely valuable, these surveys can tend to make the results appear more critical than those of a more unbiased general population.

USABILITY TESTING

Evaluating how well a system works with your users is another obvious way to collect information and identify potential challenges that users are experiencing with your product. Typically, this approach involves bringing a small number of people (usually fewer than 10) one by one into a usability lab to walk through a predefined set of tasks. The tests are normally facilitated by a usability professional who asks questions, observes the user's behavior, and at the end of the study, creates a report documenting their findings. Reflecting on Plato's cave allegory, a usability test is a lot like inviting people into your cave and asking them what they think about the shadows. That may sound like a drag on usability testing, but it isn't intended to be. Valuable insights are normally gained from usability tests. It's just very important to keep in mind that the test is being done in a controlled environment with a facilitator present—which is completely unlike how a user would actually interact with your product.

OBSERVATION AND INTERVIEWS

An alternative to having the users come to you in a lab is to gather insights in a less assumption-based, more realistic, and natural environment— outside of the cave, so to speak. We can do this by going to where our users are, to observe them on their own turf. Just like the prisoner freed from the cave, immerse yourself and take in the surroundings of your users. Leave behind any preconceived notions about how you intended your product to be used when you designed and built it. Your goal is to observe without prejudice how the user interacts with your product or service on their terms. What are they trying to achieve? Where are they when they typically use your product: at home, in a busy office, commuting on a loud and crowded train? Are they focused on the task at hand or easily and often distracted? What frustrates them about their experience? What do they value the most? Were they able to easily accomplish their task? When they're finished, how does the overall experience make them feel?

When interviewing your users, keep them focused on things that have actually happened to them instead of hypotheticals. And direct your questions around identifying pain points and jobs to be done rather than asking them to come up with creative solutions. For instance, "Tell me about a time when you became frustrated because you couldn't finish your task" will yield better results than "How could we redesign this product to make it easier for you to complete your task?"

It's you and your team's job to conceive of and deliver solutions. It's not the job of your users.

Remember that.

It's understandable that we can't always be taking field trips to go visit and observe our users. After all, there's a lot of work to be done designing, building, and testing our solutions. But we should make an attempt to do so as regularly as possible.

Set a goal to get out of the cave and spend a day or two doing site visits with customers at least once every month. Not only does this approach give you the ability to routinely observe users on their own terms, but it also allows you to get concepts for new design solutions into their hands in order to gather additional feedback.

This continual feedback loop will be very valuable as you move through the development of your product strategy and vision.

INTERNAL INTERVIEWS

When you can't regularly go spend time with your users, there's a very good chance that surrogates are available in your organization whose job involves speaking with your customers every day. Sales associates and customer service representatives are constantly having conversations with prospective and existing customers.

If you're not incorporating these members of your organization in your efforts to collect user feedback, you're most likely missing out on valuable user insights. Yes, gathering information secondhand from customer service and sales staff isn't as pure as speaking to customers directly, but it's definitely better than nothing. Additionally, you can use this as an opportunity to train your customer service and sales force on unbiased interview techniques and how best to capture customer insights and pain points.

Be sure that a balanced approach to gathering information is used. Whenever possible, it's best to deploy a wide net to capture a large and varied quantity of feedback. When you encounter customer feedback in its many forms, remember Plato and the shadows on the wall. How might we combine multiple research approaches to challenge assumptions revealed in the data? Consider assigning "confidence scores" to the user problems that you encounter.

Similar user sentiments that have been gathered from a variety of sources, combined with your teams' expert analysis and additional research, would mean a problem could be assigned a much higher confidence score than a single opinion shared via a shadowy app store review. The confidence scores have a dual benefit of clearly indicating which problems could benefit from additional validation while also allowing the product team to identify the highest-priority problems to tackle.

ON DIPLOMACY: BRINGING THE MESSAGE BACK TO THE CAVE

When we last encountered our freed prisoner from the cave allegory, he was happily exploring and embracing this newly discovered world full of sensations he'd never before experienced. After a period of time living outside of the cave, the freed prisoner, remembering his fellow cave dwellers, decides that he should return and share the wonders of his new perspective with the prisoners.

Upon reentering the cave, the freed prisoner's eyes have a hard time readjusting to the darkness after living outside in the bright sunlight. Despite his near blindness, he's able to make his way deeper into the cave and find his fellow cave dwellers. At this point, he breathlessly shares what he's discovered about the world beyond the cave. He describes the bright sunlight and the forms he encountered that are so much more real than the shadows cast on the wall. He basically explains to the cave dwellers, without presenting tangible evidence, that everything they've ever known about their lives is wrong. It's all just been an illusion.

Do you think that the rest of the cave dwellers took kindly to the message being shared with them by the freed prisoner?

Spoiler alert: They did not.

In fact, due to the freed prisoner's loss of vision, combined with his insane raving about how shadows aren't the real world—obviously due to leaving the cave (assumption!)—the rest of the cave dwellers decide that they should try to kill anyone who compels them to leave the cave. Ouch!

By and large, business leaders claim to be open to and actively seek change. They want new processes and operating models that will promote efficiency and collaboration. They want to change the corporate org structure in order to boost employee engagement. They want to launch amazing and original new products that their customers will love.

Sadly, as the cave allegory illustrates, there's a big gap between wanting change and actually being *willing* to change. In fact, like those terrified of leaving the cave, many people will fight tooth and nail to maintain the status quo. Keep this cautionary tale in mind as we explore the concept of using first principles to truly drive your product visions to new levels of innovation.

WALK THE DIPLOMATIC TIGHTROPE

Remember those annoying kids who never stop asking questions? "Why?" Because I said so. Now give me a break with the questions already! This is where the diplomacy comes in—to calm the agitated cave dwellers who want so strongly to believe in their shadows.

Start by consistently (and gently) challenging assumptions among your trusted core team members and encourage them to get into the habit as well. Simply asking "Are we making an assumption here?" is a good place to start. Once everyone is in the habit of regularly identifying assumptions versus empirical truths, introduce the team to the method of Socratic Questioning. The more you and your team use this approach, the better your results will be when verifying and framing problems.

As you and your team get better at these techniques, you'll inevitably encounter stakeholders outside of the core team who are hanging on to shared beliefs and reasoning by analogy. Ask your questions with the wonder of a child rather than in a challenging or patronizing way. Some cave dwellers may continue to resist the forms you're trying to show them, but more will see the merits of moving beyond the shadows to embrace the world outside of the cave.

LIVING OUTSIDE THE CAVE

Your evolution as a strategic designer has taken you from operating in a primarily tactical mindset—someone who makes things attractive and usable—to envisioning a bolder and brighter future for your organization and its customers. Your actions will prove that designers aren't simply focused on aesthetics. Your ability to collaborate with your team as a strategic leader will allow you to increase the level of trust and influence your business and development partners have in you. You're demonstrating the ability to empathize with end users as well as internal partners and stakeholders. All of this, along with clearly communicating a strategy-led product vision, has the power to rally the entire business around a profound and exciting new direction. And not only will you have strategic vision, you will be capable of taking the steps to achieve it. Let's get into it.

PART II
THE VISION

It's all about the product vision, the keystone of a product or service. A good vision brings a strategy's complex connections to life and clearly expresses the product's future direction. This is done by telling the story of an ideal experience and conceptually illustrating the offering's features and benefits. Three chapters cover the phases of the product vision process in detail, with help from a real-world example:

- Getting Started with the A-Team

- Strategy: Connecting the Dots

- Telling the Story of the Future Experience

CHAPTER 4
GETTING STARTED WITH THE A-TEAM

One of the most popular shows on American television in the mid-1980s was *The A-Team*. The show—which made Mr. T a superstar and was, in retrospect, awful—was about a group of Vietnam-war veterans on the run from the law for a crime they didn't commit. Each episode introduced a mission featuring a person in desperate need of the A-Team's assistance. The team, four former members of the U.S. Army Special Forces, would find their way to the person in need and develop a creative way to help (usually involving booby traps and makeshift explosives), all while evading capture from the long arm of the law. Got a problem with an unruly biker gang harassing your customers, or a crooked small-town sheriff who unjustly imprisoned your boyfriend? Bring in the A-Team!

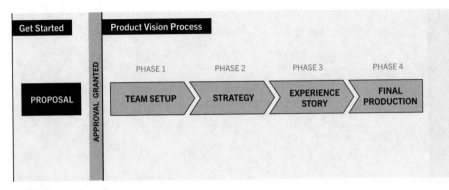

FIGURE 4.1 You Are Here, the proposal.

Each of the four members of the A-Team served a specific function in order to successfully accomplish their missions. Murdock, who had to be broken out of a mental institution before each mission, was an expert pilot who would transport the team and their gear. B. A. (which stood for bad attitude) was the mechanic, demolitions specialist, and muscle. Face was the smooth-talking con artist. Lastly, the team leader, strategist, and master of disguise was Colonel John "Hannibal" Smith, who also had the honor of saying his catchphrase in every episode: "I love it when a plan comes together."

Your teammates in product vision won't be breaking people out of medium-security prisons or assembling cabbage cannons out of duct tape and spare parts, but each team member must bring specific strengths to the important roles they play. Before the team can be assembled, you, as the strategic designer, must present a proposal that persuades the bean counters and corner-office dwellers of the value of developing a proper product vision (**Figure 4.1**). Going through a proposal exercise is important because it evaluates whether an idea is worthy of a full product vision effort and subsequently, a Visioneering endeavor.

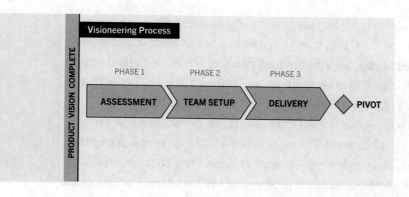

This chapter will cover the nuts and bolts of getting started and forming your team:

- Crafting the proposal

- Making the pitch

- Covering team skill sets

- Establishing the team contract, working agreement, and values

- Creating a laboratory environment

- Getting into a team rhythm

THE "GET STARTED" PROPOSAL

It's time to start preparing a proposal for a product vision when an intriguing idea either pops into your head or lands in your lap. Most commonly, an idea will come to you when your strategic design instincts kick in to detect a substantially better potential future state for an existing product, or you intuitively sense the need for an entirely new product. But what could also happen is the business will gift the designer an idea. With any gifted idea, proceed with caution. When the gift comes from a business peer, that's a great sign. They are looking at you, the strategic designer, as a collaborative partner. But, when a senior business stakeholder dangles an idea in front of you, with guaranteed funding—know that gifted idea comes with strings. It may seem like you won the lottery, but really that stakeholder is enlisting you to bring their idea to life, as they specifically imagine it (pixel for pixel) rather than asking you to evaluate and explore the idea to see if it has merit. However, when a business peer has a spark of an idea and asks you to help—dive in! This is a great sign the dynamics between design and business are progressing towards a truly collaborative partnership.

In all of these scenarios, it's important to first lay the groundwork that explains the need for a product vision. Make the argument to the decision makers that without an aspirational yet achievable endpoint in mind, any project is unlikely to reach a meaningful destination. Once this argument is successful, the concept of creating a product vision usually makes sense to everyone.

Find some trusted allies to help—maybe another designer who's a naturally innovative thinker, a developer who can speak to technical opportunities on the horizon, or a copywriter who can craft some compelling content. Get them to commit to spending a few days helping you. If necessary, however, as a strategic designer you are capable and well equipped to go it alone. Hey, forging the less taken path, solo, is nothing we designers haven't done a hundred times before. You're an adventurer with a steadfast sense of independence equipped with a superpower: the ability to envision the future. Whether you're going it solo or with a small group, it's critical that you *time-box* this proposal effort: try not to spend more than one workweek (40 hours) putting this together. One reason not to spend too much time is that you don't have backing yet, which could start you off on the wrong foot with the bean counters. Remember, the proposal is not the be-all, end-all—that's what the product vision process is for. The goal of your proposal is to get leadership to sign-off on the body of work, which can be achieved in any way that inspires trust, creates excitement and motivates the people in charge to give the green light. Any way you choose to get there, the project you propose to embark upon should

- Be transformative

- Make a difference in the lives of your customers

- Help your business achieve its goals

THE FIVE-SLIDE DECK

The five-slide deck is a useful proposal format. This five-slide deck is persuasive, inspiring, and action oriented. As you write, keep your audience (the stakeholders) top of mind. This will help with tone. It also never hurts to add a glossy cover at this stage; slather the cover in on-brand-flavored eye candy that will hook those stakeholders' attention from the start. The content on the cover should include a project description, contact information, and date.

Here are the topics of the five slides:

1. How might we do things differently?

2. Statement of intent

3. Mood board

4. Requested staff

5. Commitment

SLIDE 1: HOW MIGHT WE DO THINGS DIFFERENTLY?

The topmost slide presents the proposed idea(s) or theory. It should present a need to address with an existing product or a pitch to invent something brand-new. Label the effort as either "a serious issue" OR "a great opportunity."

Opportunity: New Product

A spark of a new product idea is undoubtedly exciting. But keep your feet planted firmly on the ground. The spark needs to be rooted in an opportunity, however loose:

- Is there an emerging market that the company could benefit from?

- Is a new demand surfacing, or is the current demand shifting?

- Has new research produced a gem of an insight into your customer base and their unmet needs?

The slide should touch on the benefit for both the target audience and the business itself. Use your unique ability to think from a user's perspective and solve those user problems (while keeping the business goals top of mind) to illustrate that you're solving for two sides of the coin. Check in with colleagues about your great idea and see whether it resonates, and whether it has already been tried. If others are excited, it might be worth pursuing.

Issue: Product Vision Deficit

Instead of undertaking a new product, you might propose to tackle an established product with *product vision deficit* (more about this in Chapter 8, "Building Your Visioneering Practice")

A product or service with product vision deficit can be easily identified. In the most obvious cases, an offering's product vision deficit stems from a lack of upfront strategy work, resulting in a flawed product vision. These products lack clear business objectives, vaguely address user problems and misalign with their company's mission. Look for the teams lost in a "feature factory," working in circles, and often carelessly heading off in any direction. More often with highly-skilled teams, product vision deficit simply means the offering has most—or even all—strategic elements addressed up front, but the team didn't then translate the strategy into a proper product vision.

SLIDE 2: STATEMENT OF INTENT

Discuss the relevance of your idea and how you intend to proceed. At a very high level, make your argument as to how the opportunity aligns with the company's North Star (mission, purpose, and brand values).

While preparing your five-slide presentation, you may be surprised to learn that the corporate mission (what your company does) and purpose (why they do it) are unclear or even left undefined. Sadly, this is more common than you might think at many large and established businesses. Do your best to gather the information; get as close as you can to defining mission and purpose by speaking to leaders throughout the business. You may hear some conflicting information coming from different members of the executive team based on their own goals and perspectives. Remember the audience for whom you're producing the presentation and do your best to align with the mission and purpose that keeps them engaged.

You may want to address past project(s) that failed in the same vein. Simply list those efforts and briefly talk to why those past efforts, while well intended, failed because of reasons x, y, and z. Explain why the company is now in a better position to succeed (because of timing, technology, or internal talent). And despite those failed efforts' shortcomings, it never hurts to give credit where it's due. Give credit to previous teams whose good thinking now benefits this new endeavor. Frame any analysis fairly, and do not—repeat, do not—throw any colleagues under the bus. Whether those contributors are still employed at the company or have since long gone, slandering others' work is a bad look and will come back to bite you.

SLIDE 3: MOOD BOARD

This slide leverages your visual communication superpower to assemble an inspirational mood board. In fact, you may want to create the content for this slide first. Showing stakeholders "What if . . . ", is a great way to pique the audience's interest and get them seeing things differently. Intended as a conversation starter, your ability to give stakeholders a glimpse into the future will have the entire room on the edge of their seats. Success will provoke endless remarks: "Oh! and what if the future of our offerings went something like this?" The mood board can show a collage of competitive offerings, cutting-edge technologies, and high-level images of potential services, interfaces, and interactions designed to deliver measurable customer and business value. Stick to your time box here, and importantly, don't overdesign this section. Your intention is to whet your audience's appetite and get them inspired to take the next step by committing to a proper vision initiative.

SLIDE 4: REQUESTED STAFF

It's time to think about who else you might enlist in your vision quest. At the end of the day, every project is at the mercy of the competence of a team and their working chemistry. An A-Team whose core members have both high expertise and working chemistry is special. That special makeup will better overcome obstacles and will collectively raise the bar—but is not so easy to come by. If you can assemble that team, most stakeholders can be persuaded to let them further investigate a fledgling idea that they themselves can't quite wrap their heads around—putting faith in the team's abilities over their own faith in the idea. Request the people you believe are a great fit for the BEDRC core roles (business, engineering, design, research, and content; more on that later in this chapter). On this slide, list each team member and a handful of bullet points to distinguish their unique attributes that qualify the individual for the intended core role on the team. Include their responsibilities and note each individual's experience level with relevant accomplishments. Alongside each person's primary role, include a supporting secondary strength. In the end, you may not get exactly the team you're requesting, but it's best to start by asking for who you believe you'll need to do the best work possible.

SLIDE 5: COMMITMENT

Now that you have stakeholders on the hook, salivating over the possibilities, it's time for the ask. Make like Cuba Gooding, Jr.'s character in Jerry McGuire: "Show. Me. The money!" Don't leave it to stakeholders to decide your project's fate. Each product vision effort asks for a commitment from stakeholders for "funding." Similar to the startup pitching investors for seed stage funding, the team will be asking for dedicated time to accomplish their goals. An acceptable time range should be anywhere between six and ten weeks, which translates to three and five sprints, with each sprint being a two-week increment. Whatever you do, don't underestimate the time needed. Also, don't forget outside costs, such as those connected to research studies. To estimate properly, evaluate both the team's level of expertise and the volume of research that needs to be done. Even a highly efficient team with exceptional skill and momentum will likely need the full 10 weeks if the project is starting from scratch with no research done.

THE PITCH

Arrange a formal meeting with the stakeholder(s) to present the proposal. In your accepted design role, you've probably had many chances to earn the trust of your product program and senior executives within your company. However, the first time you approach the creation of a product vision might be seen as stepping outside your "lane." It may sound counterintuitive, but a good way to set yourself up for success is to make in-person attendance a priority for both the presenter and the key stakeholders. Face-to-face human connection can be an invaluable asset, especially when pitching. Achieving this may mean working with each stakeholder's executive assistant to coordinate when everyone is in the same location.

Be aware that the price tag might scare off even the most open-minded leader. How can you convince your employer that putting in the hard work to assemble a strategy-driven product vision is a worthwhile investment?

Arm yourself with this book's case of the devastating effects a business will suffer due to absence of proper product vision. If you see that complete success is not in the cards that day, negotiate for a partial win, such as a trial period. Be sure to document the agreed-on decisions, no matter what the result.

PITCHING ETIQUETTE

If you are new to pitching, the first greenlight may take a few tries. Be patient, but persevere. The more you pitch ideas, the better those proposals will become. Here are a few quick scheduling wins that could tip the odds in your favor. Be mindful of the day of the week and time of day you're scheduled to pitch. On a Tuesday, that mid-morning slot should be golden. Everyone has time to settle in first thing, send emails, and then give their full attention before they tackle the rest of the week. Choosing your timing is an easy win that will set you up for success. Avoid early-morning Mondays and end-of-day Fridays, always. The stakeholders will either be just waking up or already checked out for the weekend. Lastly, be sure to avoid the week right before a big holiday or the weeks that have department conflicts such as a multiday conference.

DOCUMENTING RESULT

No matter the result, the conversation at the pitch meeting should be documented. The proposal should be amended with the stakeholders' contributions. Send the adjusted proposal to the contributing stakeholder for formal approval. You must request and secure a firm commitment to dedicated resources before the product vision work officially kicks off. Strategic designers conduct all product vision efforts *one hundred percent above board*, no exceptions. And always favor written approval with email receipt over a verbal response.

TRIAL PERIOD

Here's the rub: all stakeholders may not be so easily persuaded by the power of a strategy-led product vision. In this situation, try to convince them to sign off on a trial period. A trial period is the time required for a full product vision completing each of the four phases (see Figure 4.1). If necessary, break your work week into three or four contiguous blocks— that way, you can be flexible and fit in other projects and responsibilities, both yours and those of your stakeholders.

NOT VISION READY?

Maybe your senior leadership team isn't quite ready to invest in a fully funded product vision. Go back to basics. The most common need is to transition products from business-centric to user-centric. The digital products created by many large enterprises tend to reflect internal organizational structures and can be bloated with unnecessary features. Your initial proposal may simply be to demonstrate, "What if . . . " showing how a product could be more effective if solving customer needs took top priority. Here you are simply aiming to better understand and better focus on delivering value to customers. Challenge yourself and your fellow designers to focus on identifying opportunities and making improvements doing what they do best: interaction and interface design. Get the ball rolling by redesigning a feature that's already on the market. As an exercise, ask the team to consider whether they're truly considering the user's point of view and to think about how they could create an alternate approach:

- Are we doing what we've always done?

- Is there another way of thinking about this?

Rethink how the user interacts with the product at a high level and how you could make it more user-centric, and then present the concept to your product team. For example, suppose your company still has a website that

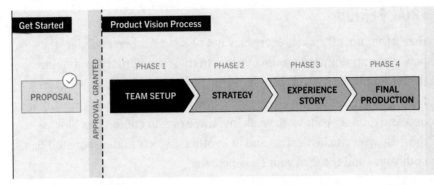

FIGURE 4.2 You Are Here, the first phase after approval: assembling your team.

resembles its organizational hierarchy chart; consider how might you get started with integrating design at a more strategic level by redesigning the website (or a section of the website or an application) to make it more user centric, and then measure the results. With each tiny victory—learning about and designing for user needs, delivering hypotheses to test solutions, and measuring how they're working—you and your fellow designers will continue building the trust and credibility needed to move towards earning your first product vision initiative.

YOUR PRODUCT VISION A-TEAM

With an approved proposal in hand, you're off and running. Now that you've successfully delivered your five-slide presentation and secured an official sign-off for the product vision engagement (even if it's only provisional), you need to pull together your A-Team and set up the project. Per the A-Team, you won't need any demolitions experts, but five key disciplines will make your team effective: the BEDRC roles (pronounced "bedrock," see **Figure 4.3**):

- Business
- Engineering
- Design
- Research
- Content

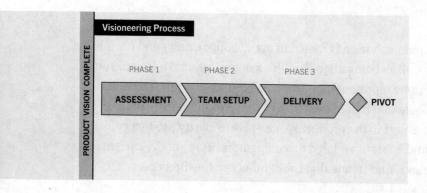

Keep in mind that just because there are five key disciplines, that doesn't mean your team will be made up of five people. You may be assigned only one or two additional people to join you in your efforts to create a product vision, in which case each person will have to wear multiple hats. This isn't ideal, but hey, do what you have to do. Perhaps a designer (yourself or a fellow designer) who once doubled as the development resource, could fill the engineering role. On the other hand, you might be able to get a large team with as many as ten people. Whatever the number of people on the team, it's important that you try to find teammates capable of filling each role.

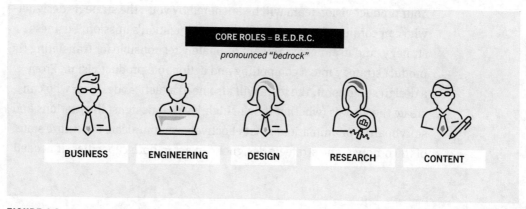

FIGURE 4.3 The BEDRC roles must be represented on your team.

BUSINESS

A successful product vision is rooted in market opportunity and business objectives as well as being aligned with an organizational mission. Your team needs strong representation from the product program's business side to contribute that half of the strategy work. Your business partner should be an expert in the product space—able to clarify product goals and understand analytics related to: competitors, usage of the current product offerings, and trends that could influence the direction your vision takes.

ENGINEERING

The engineer on the team understands and influences how you will be able to build your product vision. They should provide a candid assessment of potential technical challenges of building the product. Their role includes anticipating whether your organization's current technology stack can support it. The engineer also acts as an expert on technology trends and can help with the creation of proofs of concept and prototypes to demonstrate technical feasibility.

DESIGN

Your product vision team will be anchored by you—the strategic designer—who can connect the dots between an organization's mission, business strategy, and user needs. You are ultimately responsible for translating the product strategy into a compelling and actionable product vision. From a design standpoint, the team will also need a tactical designer who can create the visuals (whether they're high-level UI designs, illustrations and storyboards, or animations) that effectively communicate the future state of the product. The strategic designer can act in both capacities, if needed.

RESEARCH

How do you move beyond assumptions to truly understand what your target audience needs and values? How do you validate the concepts you've developed to make sure you're on the right track? You need someone on your team who understands how to conduct research that will allow you to capture these insights. Be aware that this task is not about usability research. During the strategy phase, you are seeking a deeper understanding through ethnography and contextual inquiry—uncovering pain points and providing insights into how to meet a key user need. Too often, businesses deliver products and features based solely on assumptions; "it's what we've always done; it's what our competition is doing." The research can validate or invalidate current assumptions as well as open the team's eyes to insights that go beyond incremental product improvements to the creation of brand-new markets.

CONTENT

A great vision tells a simple but compelling story about how the future state of a product will benefit your customers as well as achieve business goals. To help tell the story of the experience, you'll need someone on the team who is an expert wordsmith. Your content strategist can provide direction about the tone to use to communicate with your target audience. Effective marketing language that will eventually sell the concept to users begins by convincing internal decision makers and team members.

BE SELECTIVE!

What's the secret to form an innovative, outcome-driven team? Be patient, but selective—even picky. This work is difficult. Individuals cut out for this type of work thrive in face of challenge. They've got grit, and lots of it. The team's working chemistry should happen organically, and if it doesn't, be brave enough to cut the cord (respectfully, of course). Hopefully, you'll find a pack of people whose talents complement yours and, most important, collectively raises the bar. Once you've assembled a team that features a strong combination of these skills, it's time to determine how best to work together in a fluid, collaborative, and inquisitive environment.

TEAM CONTRACT

Each team, and the way that they work together, is unique. Once you've formed your team, make sure everyone is aligned with the team values and how team members will work together. You'll be working closely with your teammates in an environment that can be intellectually challenging and emotionally draining. As the team kicks off the work, take some time upfront to discuss what matters to each team member in terms of core values and working agreements and to begin building trust.

CORE VALUES

The team's core values make us who we are—our code of conduct and promise to one another. As our team continues to evolve and grow, these are the beliefs most important to hold fast to; core values and guiding tenets that our team leaders will hire for or fire for . . . shaping our special team's culture with good people who personify these values and put them to work every day. At the outset of a product vision effort, determine your team's core values.

➡ TRY IT THIS WAY

Here are examples of core values that might be embraced by an effective team:

- **Respect.** Honor one another's abilities, achievements, and expertise.

- **Partnership.** The sum of our strengths and different backgrounds will achieve results greater than those we can achieve alone.

- **Open-Mindedness.** We listen and consider what others have to say before expressing our own viewpoint.

- **Dependability.** We keep our word, always.

- **Disruptive at Heart.** Whether braving the more challenging path, or forging a new path, we're passionately committed to doing right by the users we serve.

- **Transparency and Candor.** We build trust within a team by communicating honestly, openly, and clearly (...and often).

WORKING AGREEMENTS

Working agreements are commonly used on *agile* teams and represent how team members arrange to work with one another. These agreements often include times of day when team members are available to meet versus when they're actively working, communication standards (for example: use video if meeting remotely or document new research findings in the team Slack channel), and general rules of engagement for how to productively interact and work with one another.

TRUST

Above all, your team must work to embrace the concept of psychological safety. Developing a product vision is a risky endeavor; it requires people to go out on a limb and out of their comfort zone. A great vision represents a bold change, and change—though the only constant—has a way of frightening people. Change is inherently uncomfortable. It's different from the status quo. Your team must always foster a safe environment where people are allowed to be vulnerable and feel comfortable revealing their authentic selves. Only in this environment, where team members are free to be candid with one another, allowed to take risks, and reminded that it's perfectly acceptable—even encouraged—to be wrong, will truly transformative ideas emerge. Psychological safety must be cultivated within a team. It requires time to allow people to truly get to know one another and

DESIGNING INSIDE THE BOX

What's the importance of building trust within a team focused on creating a product vision?

On the teams I have worked with, I've found that while there are a myriad of factors that determine the effectiveness of a team, teams composed of individuals that feel safe to be themselves and aligned around their purpose tend to consistently produce value and desired outcomes. At their core, two areas offer a great place to start when reflecting on the levels of trust and safety in your team(s):

First: behavior modeling should be at the core of what your team does. The culture of any social group is determined by the sum of its composites. It is for this reason that everyone should have the space to be an authentic leader. If you want an environment where people call out things as they notice them, the environment must be stable and safe enough for them to do so. Anyone can be a leader at different points in time; leveraging these value-adds as they manifest ensures innovations that may happen do in fact happen.

Second: create a learning-driven environment. Contrary to the way that many systems are set up, failure is not actually failing . . . make sure there is precedence and space on the team for people to take risks safely. Your main priority should be to set up conditions that allow for learning, where the team can clearly identify significant results regardless of whether they are positive or negative. The worst outcome is one where results are inconclusive because in those cases nothing is learned, ergo nothing is gained. Additionally, with most experiments, failures or negative results are oftentimes more significant than positive results, as they help you hone in on what you are working to achieve. It is for this reason that it's very important that people are given the space to take risks and fail.

—CHISARA NWABARA
PRODUCT & SERVICE DESIGN STRATEGIST I AGILE TRANSFORMATION LEAD
WWW.CHISOLOGY.COM

build relationships in order to create empathy and trust. It takes only one team member who's unwilling to lower their guard to negatively impact the harmony of the entire team. It's best to identify and remove these team members as soon as possible. Diplomatically removing a teammate who has the potential to disrupt team harmony—even if they're a brilliant teammate—will result in a more productive team and a better end product in the long run.

A LABORATORY ENVIRONMENT

If possible, request a sizable, dedicated team room for the duration of the product vision engagement. Equip this space with comfy chairs, whiteboards, a big monitor, and video/audio conferencing. For added ambience, include posters, snacks and refreshments, a coffee machine, thinking putty that you hold and squish, and a Bluetooth speaker to pump out the team's shared playlist. Nothing like some fresh coffee and inspirational music to keep the team motivated.

CO-LOCATION

Product vision work requires a very close design–business alliance. It will be up to you, as the strategic designer, to stamp out the barriers that persist between business associates and creatives. Achieving this can only be done when you are physically in the same place. Make the effor to work co-located at least part of the time. When co-located, you'll learn to speak one another's language, collaboratively make decisions, and be wiser at choosing battles. At some point, between working lunches and trust falls, watch the business convert to this new way of doing things. Gaining carte blanch visibility over the business wall—revealing the motivations and intricacies of the respective business strategy that is shaping your product vision. The realization of how to work with your strategic business counterparts is success in itself.

DIGITAL VS. ANALOG

Your project space is a physical (or part-time virtual) space where the team meets on a regular basis to collaborate, brainstorm, debate, and share research findings. The space should be equipped with a large whiteboard and plenty of room to hang critical information that will guide your team's decisions. The idea is to curate an environment where the team can work without distraction and be immersed in their understanding of the target audience, product space, and business goals.

TRANSPARENCY

Transparency will serve any team well—especially those working on a product vision. Not only will it help build team members' skill to connect the dots gathered through their research, but it will also give stakeholders the ability to understand how the team is conducting their work. The more your team can be open with their process and how they arrive at decisions they're making, the more they can build trust with upper management who gave the green light to do the work in the first place. Your team room is a safe space for your team to work and share ideas. It's also a lab where people can observe experiments taking place in real time.

➡ TRY IT THIS WAY

Do to foster transparency:

- Transparency works in our favor. Have an open-door policy to share work in progress.

- Schedule stand-ups (see the next section) in the room, schedule core hours, and the rest is revolving door. Carve out your own quiet time each day, somewhere else. Maybe at your own desk, a coffee shop, or at home?

- Maintain regular coffee breaks and lunch with coworkers outside the vision project.

- Keep a simple written whiteboard with weekly to-do's current. Tape up high-level accomplishments to a wall for at-a-glance progress that anyone can read.

Don't undermine transparency:

- Make the team room a closed-door clubhouse. When you find yourself working in large groups, alongside hundreds of people, it can give off a vibe of exclusivity.

- Spend the whole day in the team room.

- Spend the whole working day with just the product vision or Visioneering team.

- Give selected coworkers the inside scoop. The game of telephone will quickly get word back to a stakeholder before they've been updated themselves.

WORKING TOGETHER AS A TEAM

Along the same lines as determining team values and working agreements, your team should develop a rhythm that works best for all team members collectively. This course of action will include how information is collected and distributed among the team, as well as the cadence of regular team communications, check-ins, and stakeholder reviews. The following chapters will provide more specifics about how the team will go about developing and validating the strategy and product vision. In the meantime, here are some general best practices for effectively working together as a vision team.

COMMUNICATION STANDARDS

Set up regular team *stand-up meetings*, which are kept short by intent: no one sits down. Each team member can share what they worked on since the last meeting, reveal what they plan to work on next, and discuss any blockers limiting their ability to complete their work. Stand-ups aren't intended to be deep dives into the work being done; they should be fairly quick meetings that enable everyone on the team to know what's being worked on, and what's most important for them to be focusing on at the moment, and for uncovering any impediments that need to be removed.

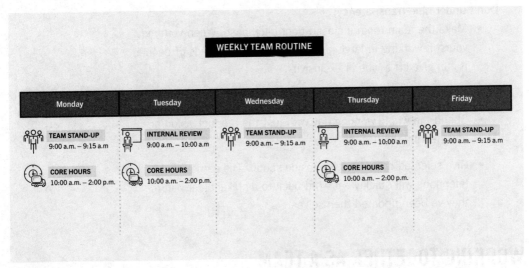

FIGURE 4.4 A typical routine includes open time as well as set meeting and working times.

You can spend 15 minutes each day doing a stand-up meeting, or you may decide to run your stand-ups less frequently (1–3 times per week) if the information being shared becomes redundant. Schedule a cadence that works for your team. Part of your stand-up meetings on Mondays should include an overview of the week's priorities. Write those priorities on a whiteboard for the entire team to see, and mark them off when they are complete. Don't forget to celebrate your accomplishments along the way, even if it seems as trivial as marking something off your team to-do list.

You can see in **Figure 4.4** that most of Wednesday and Friday are intentionally left open for team members to focus independently on their work as needed. This "open time" may include collaborating with additional teams or focusing on other projects or administrative work.

INTERNAL REVIEWS

An internal review or working session—where each team member can take time to go deeper into the work that they've done, share research findings, plan for upcoming activities, brainstorm, and wordsmith presentations— should take place on a regular basis. These sessions may happen informally on an ad hoc basis if the team is spending most of their time together in a shared team room. Regardless, it's a good idea to get time on the calendar—at least once a week—to make sure the team is coming together to plan, share, and discuss what they're working on.

Core hours are a reserved block of time where all team members plan on being available to work alongside one another. During these protected blocks of time, teams should plan to be present and work together in the team room. Remote team members can make sure they're available and online through chat or video. Don't feel as if you need to plan an agenda or specific action items that will be worked on during core hours (unless you want to make sure the team is focused on completing a specific goal). This time is dedicated to team discussion and collaboration. Avoid scheduling and attending meetings unrelated to the work being done by the vision team during core hours (for example, meetings related to another project or team).

STAKEHOLDER CHECK-INS

When you delivered your pitch to senior leadership to form the product vision team, you should have agreed to regular check-ins with senior stakeholders. It may sound counterintuitive, but the more regularly your team is sharing progress with senior stakeholders, the better. Try to keep these reviews informal and conversational; invite stakeholders to your regularly scheduled review meetings whenever possible. Avoid turning review sessions into more work for your team, such as spending additional time creating presentations to review with stakeholders. The goal is to keep senior leaders aware of what you're doing and give them the opportunity to provide input and insights along the way.

GET OUTSIDE!

Lastly, make sure you're not spending all of your time in your team room. To create a great product vision for your customers, you'll need to get out of the building and go to where your customers are! Plan times with your team that don't conflict with your core hours to get out and do interviews and conduct observational research with your target audience.

READY, SET, GO!

Although it may feel like you've won by getting to this point, there's no time to rest on your laurels. The hard work (and fun) is truly about to begin. Fortunately, you're set up for success. Expectations are clear, ideas are percolating, and your product vision A-Team has been assembled to start delivering on the promise of a transformative idea. No pressure!

CHAPTER 5

STRATEGY: CONNECTING THE DOTS

In this chapter you—the strategic designer—will learn to successfully navigate and captain the second phase of the product vision process: *strategy* (**Figure 5.1**).

No pressure, but if your strategy doesn't come together, everything that follows is at risk. This is the time to connect the dots, a laborious undertaking and not for the easily dissuaded. Be aware that a novice team may become frustrated trying to get out of the strategy gate. Don't be discouraged. If you're doing it right, the strategy can feel like David Bowie forcing your team to solve his research *Labyrinth* with no shortage of goblins, trapdoors, and riddles. Your team will be working hard to yield the key insights that you are searching for. For some, the first few weeks may not yield any obvious progress at all. Keep at it. Eventually, the accumulated information, data, and whiteboard working sessions will start to look like a pile of related puzzle pieces. And, if you're paying attention, the key insights will slowly reveal themselves and magnetically connect to form a unified whole, revealing the way to an achievable and *innovative* product vision. Because honestly, if your team is not striving toward a product vision that is innovative, then why bother?

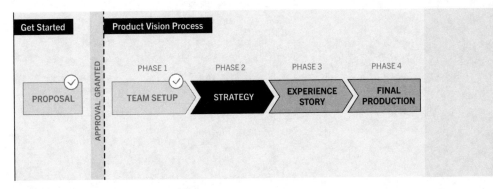

FIGURE 5.1 You are here, strategy, phase 2.

This persistent pressure to stay one step ahead of competitive disruption to the status quo should be enough to remind all of us that the time to try a new approach and embrace change is now. Competition is fierce. There's a good chance that your competitors—the sizable, established businesses you're very familiar with as well as the ones that are still small startups flying under the radar—are imminently preparing to launch a new version of their product or a brand-new offering that will upend the market landscape. A former colleague at a large financial services firm lived in fear of waking up to learn that one of the tech giants (e.g., Amazon, Facebook, Google) had entered the finance space. He knew that having to compete with mega-tech firms that had limitless funding, terabytes upon terabytes of user data, and the talent and corporate culture to quickly launch and iterate on their product offerings could completely transform the way people invested their money.

Here's a quick litmus test to tell whether you're actually pushing the envelope: comfort level. If the strategy you're outlining makes you feel relatively relaxed, then it's probably not innovative. After all, if it was easy, everybody would be doing it. Innovation carries risk, and though working in that space can be new and exciting, it is rarely comfortable. So stay vigilant, don't fool yourself into complacency and most important, get *uncomfortable.*

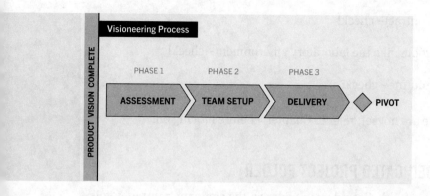

This chapter introduces the five building blocks of strategy and explains how your team will gather data, analyze patterns, and synthesize insights. You'll assemble the strategy into a presentation deck. But before we jump into strategy, you need to set up the logistics of the project, documents, ownership, and sharing.

SETUP AND LOGISTICS

As discussed in the Chapter 4, "Getting Started with the A-Team," you will have secured a firm commitment that allocates funding and dedicated resources before this first phase of the product vision process officially kicks off. Again, you must secure a formal commitment before the work begins. Believing in the value of product vision work, and further trusting in the designer to pull off this feat, will sit outside the typical comfort zone for traditional business stakeholders. But this work is—and by accounts we strategic designers are—worthy of the privilege of this type of trust. So, hold your senior stakeholder accountable to this new way of working. With the approval signed and sealed, the designer is in charge of setting up the team's needs.

- Team—check!

- Assigned stakeholders—check!

- Team contract—check!

- Team room, aka the laboratory environment—check!

- Team routine—check!

If any of these are not set, refer to Chapter 4 before moving on.

CREATE A DEDICATED PROJECT FOLDER

You should set up a dedicated team folder on the company's intranet, following this format: Create six subfolders and label one for each of the five strategic building blocks: the where, the who, the what, the when, the why (**Figure 5.2**). Label the last folder *product vision*. A seventh optional folder serves as an archive folder (for those of us who are hoarders and save everything). The master *strategy presentation* source file lives at the root of the project folder. A text file that contains such information as the best person to contact, relevant dates, a change log, and additional intranet links is also helpful.

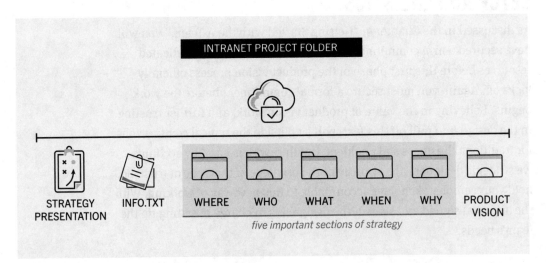

FIGURE 5.2 Intranet project folder.

THE PRESENTATION TEMPLATE

The strategy is delivered as a presentation. This deliverable reminds the established business of their past startup glory days; the format takes strong cues from the pitch deck the founders may have used with initial investors. You should set up this file as a template, creating placeholder slides for each section. Be sure to use a file format that everyone can easily access and use. Most established businesses love all things Microsoft Office, making cloud-based Word and PowerPoint applications the front runners.

Although each section is significant, the content should be concise. Include only the minimum amount of information needed to support the point, no more than two to three slides per section. If necessary, place additional supporting content at the end in an appendix. In addition to the five building blocks, don't forget the cover and the team section. Keep the up-to-date master version of this file at the root level of your dedicated intranet project folder.

Here is the structure of the presentation, with the five important sections in bold:

Cover

Table of Contents

Strategic Building Block 1: Where

Strategic Building Block 2: Who

Strategic Building Block 3: What

Strategic Building Block 4: When

Strategic Building Block 5: Why

The Team

Appendix

ESTABLISH PRESENTATION DECK CO-OWNERS

It's just common sense that more than one person should co-own a major document like the master strategy presentation deck. Aside from checks and balances, multiple owners ease the pressure of responsibility (balancing life and work). On a product vision project, the co-owners are the business partner and the strategic designer. For each section of the strategy, designate one of you as the author and the other, the editor. But know all team members filling the BEDRC (business, engineering, design, research, and content) core roles should have access and editing privileges as needed.

MANAGING UP: THE STAKEHOLDER

Developing a positive relationship with your senior stakeholder—right from the get-go—is important. The stakeholder wields the power to make or break your project. So, before the strategy starts, sit down with your stakeholder(s) and set expectations. This is the time to manage up. Schedule a private weekly one-on-one meeting. Your 1:1 meeting is a time for the stakeholder to express any concerns they may have, apart from the audience of the larger team. Nothing can tank a team's morale like an unfiltered stakeholder on the tear. Familiarize them with the overall process and the team's weekly routine. The stakeholder should not be seeing the strategy for the first time at the final presentation. Early in the process, the team will begin sharing progress with the stakeholder. Go over how weekly reviews work, what's expected from the stakeholder during a review, and give examples of constructive feedback versus ineffective criticism. At every check-in review, raise concerns of any roadblocks and assign action items to stakeholders. Don't be vague on deadlines.

Now let's dig into the details of the content that informs your product strategy.

THE STRUCTURE OF THE STRATEGY

This analogy is worth memorizing:

> *If your product vision is the keystone of any product or service,*
> *your strategy is the masonry.*

Masonry is the craft of making a solid whole out of components. All components must fit together and interlock. During the strategy phase, you work through each strategic component (a building block) and go back as needed until a solid foundation exists. The product vision, your keystone, will be the central element that locks and secures the strategy in place.

THE STRATEGIC BUILDING BLOCKS

The individual components within your masonry are the five strategic building blocks: the where, who, what, when, and why.

The following explains the way the strategic building blocks fit together—a perfect fusion of the three product disciplines that are business, design, and engineering.

Identify an opportunity space (the where) that will create measurable value for the target user (the who). The solution (the what) lives at the intersection of the where and the who, creating a mutually beneficial relationship by meeting the needs of both the business and the target audience. Predict the timing (the when) of the technology that would help execute the best experience. Finally, clarify how this offering will further the company's mission and achieve measurable business objectives (the why).

The entirety of the strategy phase is dedicated to defining and fleshing out each of the five strategic building blocks. The test of whether a block is complete is the strength of its adherence to the whole.

Try not to get hung up on the *how* at this point. After you define the strategy, the next phase of the process outlines the how at a high level. Additional detail will be clarified during the visioneering process when Scrum teams start building their product backlogs. More on that in Chapter 7, "Setting Your Compass to the North Star."

The approach to strategy is the same whether you're creating a net new product or addressing an existing product with product vision deficit. An offering with product vision deficit can be easily identified. In the most obvious cases, that offering has neither up-front strategy work nor a product vision. These products lack clear business objectives, may or may not address user problems, and could be misaligned with their company's mission. A telltale sign to look for are teams lost in "feature factories," unable to articulate why their work matters, working in circles, and often carelessly heading off in any direction. With talented teams, deficit simply means the attention to strategy fell a little bit short. Or perhaps the team addressed all of the strategic elements but didn't go on to the next phase to translate the strategy into a proper product vision. More on retrofitting a live product with product vision deficit in Chapter 8, "Building Your Visioneering Practice."

GATHER, ANALYZE, SYNTHESIZE

As the team makes their way through each of the strategic building blocks (where, who, what, when, and why), follow a structured method within each block. The approach to carving out each block involves three steps: gather, analyze, and synthesize (**Figure 5.3**).

The abridged version of this effort (additional detail on how to approach each building block follows later in this chapter) begins with the first strategic building block, the *where*, identifying an opportunity space. In

Step 1, the team gathers all the research and relevant information, keen to evaluate and fill in the gaps. In Step 2, the gathered materials are analyzed to glean patterns and findings that surface key insights. In Step 3, those key insights are synthesized into the strategy presentation. The three steps repeat for the block, until the team is confident in the definition. Then, the team moves on to the second block, the *who*, and repeats the steps. They proceed in sequence: the where, the who, the what, the when, and the why. Each block will build on the findings of the previous block. However, don't be surprised if the findings on one block inspire adjustments and tweaks to the previous block or blocks. Each new discovery will cause a ripple effect—or sometimes a tsunami—through your team's understanding of how everything connects. This is exactly as it should be. The entire strategy is complete when all the blocks interlock to form a unified, connected whole. Pace the team with a sense of urgency, but factor in time for rethinking and retooling. This is the time to get it right—as best as you can. Until the strategy comes together, your team should not move on to the next phase.

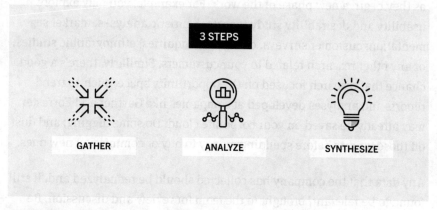

FIGURE 5.3 The three steps: gather, analyze, and synthesize.

GATHERING RESEARCH

To define the product strategy, you'll need to start by answering each of those critical building block questions: where, who, what, when, and why. Getting to the answers requires a variety of research tools and techniques. Like an investigator assembling evidence from numerous sources to build a case—conducting eyewitness interviews; arranging timelines; gathering forensic, documentary, and digital evidence—your team will review existing research and commission new studies to make the case for the product strategy.

REVIEW EXISTING RESEARCH

At the beginning of the process, the team, led by your research associate (the R in BEDRC), will sift through all relevant research the company has already obtained or conducted about the who and the where. You are looking for existing research related to this work (or an earlier iteration of it) with regard to your target audience that can be shared with your team as they begin a new phase of the work. For example, you may explore usability and desirability study reports, heuristic analyses, market segmentation, customer surveys, contextual inquiries, ethnographic studies, or any other research related to your customers. Similarly, there's a good chance that research focused on the opportunity space, such as trend reports and analyses developed at companies like Gartner and Forrester, may already be saved on your corporate cloud. Do some digging, and dust off those reports before spending money to buy or commission new ones.

Any data that the company has collected should be reanalyzed and, if still found to be relevant, brought to the team for review and discussion. Be on the lookout for research gems that have been discarded, dismissed, or overlooked. Most businesses have a treasure trove of abandoned studies and reports, directly or tangentially related to the work your team is doing, waiting to be discovered—often results of projects that happened before your time.

After collecting and sifting through what your team has on hand, determine which of the available research is helpful, highlight areas that deserve more attention, and note any gaps that need to be filled with newly commissioned studies or reports.

NEW RESEARCH OPPORTUNITIES

After reviewing and analyzing the research already on hand, it's time for the team to determine what still needs to be learned about the users, the target market, and your competitors. Do blind spots exist that would benefit from the collection of additional information? Is the latest competitive analysis more than a couple of years old? Perhaps the most recent audience segmentation you have on hand was conducted prior to a market shift that could have a large impact on user sentiment and behavior. It would make sense to commission an update.

In most cases primary research (research done directly by your team versus research conducted by an external third party) will gather the most useful insights. Nothing beats getting unfiltered information firsthand, directly from your research subjects. Before proceeding with your own research, ensure that your stakeholders are made aware of any associated costs and impacts to the schedule. Though some studies could last several weeks or months, research doesn't always have to be especially costly and time consuming. Here are a couple ways to gather useful information without overextending your budget and timeline.

Optimize your analytics

If your team is focused on retrofitting an existing product with strategy and respective product vision, there may be an opportunity to improve the data that's being captured about how users are currently using the product that's in market today. Determine what, if any, data is currently being collected with regard to the number of active users, the most common user flows, the amount of time users are spending with your product, the number of actions taken by users, and so forth. Too often, especially in less mature product organizations, analytics aren't used to their full potential.

Several analytics programs are available that can be installed relatively easily within existing software products. In addition to basic traffic data (number and frequency of users and visits), you can find programs that offer heatmapping, eye tracking, and the ability to solicit direct user feedback about their experience. Before deciding which program to use to collect user data, make sure you're clear about the most important information that your team wants to capture. Tracking users through an experience to identify common entry points, paths, and potential road-blocks is often very informative.

Depending on the volume of users your current product has, you may be able to capture quite a bit of valuable data in a relatively short amount of time. Just be aware that the information being captured is raw data that will need to be interpreted, a process that can introduce bias and assumptions. An additional layer of qualitative research—speaking directly with users to put the raw data into context—is often extremely valuable coupled with your data analytics.

Contextual inquiry

Another highly insightful, yet inexpensive and nimble, form of research is the contextual inquiry. This method involves one or two researchers (often an interviewer and a notetaker) who directly observe users in the context of their natural environment. Contextual inquiry is an effective technique for studying how users interact with existing products in their natural surroundings, but it can also be especially informative for understanding user needs when a product doesn't currently exist.

If your team is conducting research on a highly complicated problem space—for example, something that may currently require many steps and multiple participants and that consumes a great deal of time like doing financial planning, choosing the right college, or purchasing a home— contextual inquiry can be illuminating. The value of this type of research is in the name: context. When you bring people into a usability lab, they're on your turf. They're performing tasks and answering questions based on a predetermined path, and usually they're trying to please or impress the person conducting the test. It's human nature. During a contextual inquiry, the participants are in a familiar space (complete with all of their life's natural interruptions) and ideally conducting themselves as they normally would. After making sure the user is comfortable, the research-er's job is to observe and to unobtrusively ask questions from time to time to help create a better understanding of the user's actions and motivations. Prompts like "Show me how you might do the following . . . " coupled with seeking to understand why a user may have taken an action or made a decision will provide worthwhile insights.

As long as you have direct access to your target audience, this type of research doesn't have to be time consuming. Your team could realistically develop the interview, schedule participants, and do the research within two to three weeks. Cost-wise, compensating participants for their time is customary, and you may have some travel expenses depending on where the interviews take place.

RESEARCH RED FLAGS

Be wary of research done on behalf of lobbying stakeholders with a lot to lose. Look out for two types of stakeholder interference: those stake-holders whose hand stirs the study pot—baking in questions that lead the witness to the preferred answer. The second, more common occurrence is the stakeholder who, post study, may skew the output to generate insights that lean in their favor. This happens more than you'd think in estab-lished businesses. Powerful stakeholders hedge their leadership roles, reputations, and bonuses on assumptions that your research will have to validate.

STRATEGIC BUILDING BLOCK 1: WHERE

Strategy building starts with the *where*. The strategy work hinges on identifying an opportunity space. Opportunity is gauged by checking the pulse of your respective industry, current market(s), and demand. You, the strategic designer, lean on the expertise of the business partner to take the lead defining your first strategic building block.

NOTES ON OPPORTUNITY

Let's keep it real. Designers do not fully appreciate the immense amount of work that goes into defining this first strategic building block. Often not even wanting to get involved with product strategy until they address the customer: who you serve, advocate, and design for. This attitude must change. You, the strategic designer, may not be leading this section of work, but you do have to support your business partner. That means you should be able to have an intelligent conversation on this topic. As the bridge that connects design to business, you will have to hone your business savvy to understand industry, market, and demand. Here are high-level notes on how this all works.

A market is a space where transactions take place—where buying and selling meet. The two players in a market space are basically the customer and the company. The company is the maker of the offering and may directly sell it to the customer, but it may also contract out the means of distribution via retailers. A new market is sparked by demand, the economic principle that is the measurement of a need or a want. A company creates an offering (the product or service) to fill demand. The concept of supply and demand expresses the relationship between the quantity of offering available, how badly people want to buy that offering, and the price people are able to pay. The law is intuitive. Supply goes up, costs go down, demand rises—because the goods become more affordable, they become more appealing. Supply goes down, costs go up, demand takes a hit. An industry is created when two or more companies are related by what they offer and compete to address demand in a market. These industry peer companies are each other's competition. They meet in the market space with their differing products in tow, vying for those customer dollars. Industry follows the ebb and flow of markets. Markets follow the ebb and flow of demand. If demand dries up, so can the respective industry.

WHERE: GATHER, ANALYZE, SYNTHESIZE

Your business partner will gather the likes of industry analyses, competitive analyses, market analyses, and so forth. They will look to understand the entire space in terms of defining the spread of competition—both indirect and direct—and establish some guardrails. The outermost boundaries are marked by the competitive offerings that innovatively push the limits. Once the team can clearly see the industry space as it currently exists, the markets in play, and the demand driving it all, they can carve out interesting opportunities.

SLIDES: [TO BE DETERMINED]

Because this is *The Designer's Guide to Product Vision* and not *The Business Partner's Guide to Product Vision*, we leave this section of the presentation to the business partner's discretion.

Heads up: Know that your business partner may have a bad habit of needing an excessive number of slides and unnecessary details to convey their point. Here are ways the designer can help. Hold them to simplifying the content and synthesizing the findings down to only a handful of key slides. To help keep the slide count to a minimum, audit the content down to its "cleanest" form. You know the drill: identify the information that conveys the core message and remove any surrounding clutter. Rinse, repeat. You can also help visualize the content. For example, a slide that speaks to a market landscape can be visualized on an x-y axis, or a slide that speaks to industry highlights could leverage spot illustrations or typography to support each statistic.

STRATEGY BUILDING BLOCK 2: WHO

Who is the *who*? The who is everything; your beloved target user is who you serve, advocate, and design for. You wouldn't blink twice if asked to go to bat for your user! But the who is a point of contention for the established business. The wants of the company often take precedence over the needs of the user. This is frustrating to designers and perpetuates the rift between business and design. This is the time to educate your business partners on the importance—and benefit—of solving for both sides of the equation.

NOTES ON ALL THINGS CUSTOMER

As the strategic designer, you should be able to have an intelligent conversation about the dynamic layers of the *who*—layers that are often missed. The audience that a company serves can include both the target customer and respective consumer as well as influencers and partners. All of these parties are often referred to by the umbrella term *user*.

Customer and consumer are two terms that are often used interchangeably but mean different things. The *customer* is the purchaser of the product and engages in the transaction with the company or a third party on behalf of the company. An influencer may have persuaded the customer to make the purchase. The customer and influencer are typically the focus of the business model. The *consumer* is the end user of the product. A customer can also be the consumer, and a consumer can be an influencer, but the consumer doesn't necessarily have to be the customer. For example, a physician (the influencer) may write a prescription for a medication that a parent (the customer) should buy for their sick child (the consumer).

Partners are another type of user. Partners encompass a variety of roles related to how a business markets and distributes their offerings. Many businesses don't provide access directly to their products and services; they work with multiple partners to help facilitate sales. In the example of a doctor writing a prescription, pharmaceutical companies that produce medications in the United States rely on partners like the U.S. Food and Drug Administration, insurance companies, and pharmacies to test, help consumers pay for, and appropriately distribute their products.

When defining the who, you must be specific about the various audiences for whom you're developing your strategy and how their roles may affect each other via a journey map depicting the overall user experience.

WHO: GATHER, ANALYZE, SYNTHESIZE

Identify the relevant audience research that's already been done and gather all available data on the customer base. You want to acquire both the raw data and the interpreted output. By obtaining the raw data, you can reanalyze the findings and confirm that the interpretation was done correctly and fairly. No biases or assumptions made here! What you are looking for is existing qualitative and quantitative studies, empathy maps, personas, customer segmentation, archetypes, user flows, customer journey maps, and problem statements from other related projects.

SLIDE: THE TARGET AUDIENCE

This first all-important slide clearly defines the user(s) for whom you are delivering this work. At the very least, provide a description of the target audience, their needs as they relate to this initiative, and any relevant information that will help your team understand and build empathy with the user. **Figure 5.4** shows an example.

Ideally, you'd want to go deeper to include an empathy map and do so for all key user types. Empathy maps capture and communicate information about users' behavior and attitudes toward a particular product, service, or experience in general. They're broken into four quadrants that contain details about what a specific user or aggregate representative persona is saying, thinking, doing, and feeling with respect to the experience that

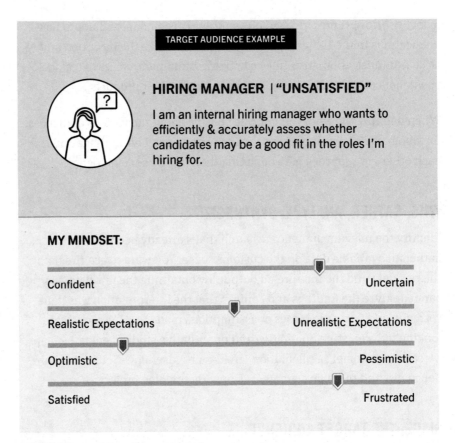

FIGURE 5.4 Target audience example.

you're studying. Empathy maps should be generated by interviewing your target audience, by observing their behavior, or via programs that gather and analyze customer feedback, collecting quotes and insights to populate the quadrants.

For example, when observing a usability session of an e-commerce check-out flow, you may take note of verbatim quotes from users. For example, the participant says out loud, "Man, this is frustrating! I would like to do this quickly, but . . . " Probe them about what they're thinking during the process without filtering their words. "Am I dumb for not seeing this?" is not a stupid response but an extremely helpful one. Observe the actions they take. Perhaps the user clicked the deactivated buy button three times; now extract how the experience of using that product made them feel—confident, satisfied, frustrated, etc. Insights can be gleaned via qualitative and quantitative research, and empathy maps can represent one person or a representative sample of similar users. Most important, the information should come directly from your target audience rather than from anecdotes and assumptions made by the team.

In addition to building empathy for the users and aligning team members on users' attitudes toward your product or service, empathy maps are a treasure trove of user problems. If you have the time, highlight and prioritize ways that alleviate user frustrations and save those for later. We will touch on them in the next chapter, "Telling the Story of the Future Experience," as we craft the experience story. And later, in Chapter 7, we will transform that list into a smaller subset of actionable problem statements that the team can use to create testable solution hypotheses.

SLIDE: CUSTOMER JOURNEY MAP

A customer journey map helps you understand more about your users (the who) in the context of your product and service offerings. Journey maps visualize the steps taken by users to achieve a particular goal, where the process is meeting or exceeding expectations, and the potential challenges and pain points that they encounter along the way.

The perspective of your journey map will vary depending on the strategy your team is developing. But given that you're most likely tasked with developing a longer-term product strategy and vision, the journey map should reflect that. In other words, your instinct may be to map the steps of a narrow use case, like an e-commerce checkout flow. Think bigger and zoom out to include a broader view of the overall customer experience. Going broad may move you outside of your intended market (the where) but will add the right amount of perspective to the journey map. Zooming out can provide additional insights that you hadn't considered. Identifying these insights and user pain points helps the team uncover actionable problems related to the process, a critical step to understanding how to deliver solutions that will matter to your users.

A final note on journey mapping: This may sound obvious, but make sure that the journey maps being developed by your team are grounded in research—you know, that part where you're actually talking to people outside of the office. Too often, businesses create journey maps based on internal assumptions and biases without validating the steps and pain points with their users through firsthand qualitative or quantitative research. Assumption-based journey maps can inject a considerable amount of risk into the product vision developed by your team. **Figure 5.5** shows an example of a customer journey map.

SLIDE: THE PROBLEM

Before diving into the nuts and bolts of writing problem statements, let's clarify the semantics of the word *problem* so that you're not put off by the negative connotation of the word. A problem in the sense of a strategy isn't necessarily harmful to the person. The user problems that we tend to focus on from a design standpoint are more akin to scientific or mathematical problems.

The problems we're identifying have a strong relationship to "Jobs" in the Jobs-To-Be-Done Framework. They may be tasks a person needs to complete or impediments to goals they want to achieve. Often defining a user problem can focus on ways to make a process more convenient, simpler, or more effective. Problems can be large, such as "Help me save for retirement." Problems can be small, like "I can't find the Submit button." Either way, user problem statements will articulate a user need without telegraphing a solution. For the purposes of a strategy phase and product vision, you're almost certain to be focusing on problems that are larger in scope than minor usability issues.

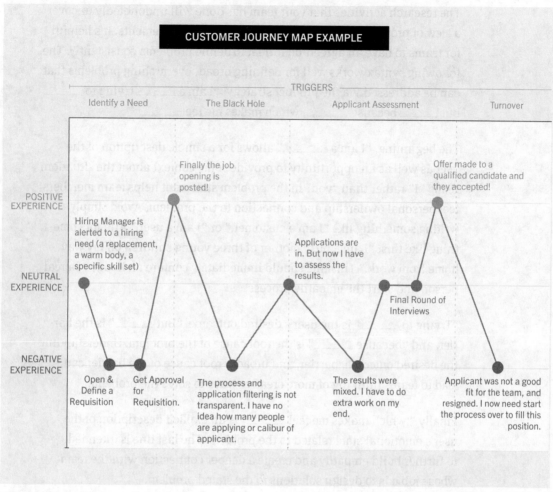

CUSTOMER JOURNEY MAP EXAMPLE

TRIGGERS

Identify a Need   The Black Hole   Applicant Assessment   Turnover

POSITIVE EXPERIENCE

NEUTRAL EXPERIENCE

NEGATIVE EXPERIENCE

Hiring Manager is alerted to a hiring need (a replacement, a warm body, a specific skill set)

Finally the job opening is posted!

Offer made to a qualified candidate and they accepted!

Applications are in. But now I have to assess the results.

Final Round of Interviews

Open & Define a Requisition

Get Approval for Requisition.

The process and application filtering is not transparent. I have no idea how many people are applying or calibur of applicant.

The results were mixed. I have to do extra work on my end.

Applicant was not a good fit for the team, and resigned. I now need start the process over to fill this position.

FIGURE 5.5 Customer journey map example.

The research activities that your team has done will undoubtedly uncover a slew of problems that can be written as problem statements. It's helpful for teams to have an agreed-on format to define problems consistently. The following syntax works well for defining broad, overarching problems that can be addressed via the product strategy: "I am a _____ trying to _____ but _____ because _____, which makes me feel _____."

The beginning, "I am a _____," allows for a simple description of the user as well as an opportunity to provide some context about the situation. Using "I" rather than "you" in the problem statement helps team members feel personal ownership and connection to the problem. Avoid simply writing something like "I am a customer," or "I am a user." Aim for something like this: "I am a busy mother of three young children on my way home from work." This line should immediately conjure an image of a real person and start the empathy process.

"Trying to _____" is the user's desired outcome. "But _____" is the barrier, and "because _____" is the root cause of the problem. Understanding the desired outcome, barrier, and broader root cause of the barrier can lead to teams thinking of more creative ways to solve the problem.

Finally, "which makes me feel _____" is an explicit description of the user's emotional state related to the problem. The last line is intended to further build empathy and create a deeper connection with the team whose job it is to design solutions to the stated problem.

For example, this is the problem statement for our "uncertain" persona, defined in the previous target user slide:

I am . . . a busy hiring manager at a large company.

Trying to . . . hire the most qualified new employees for my organization.

But . . . it's difficult to determine how well someone might fit in and succeed at our company based on their resume and a few job interviews.

Because . . . I have additional managerial responsibilities, and my time spent on hiring decisions is limited.

Which makes me feel . . . uncomfortable, like hiring great people is a bit of a crap shoot—putting my company at risk by not securing the best talent.

Avoid including too much detail when developing your problem statements. The longer they get, the less effective they can be. Be prepared to spend a lot of time getting the words and length just right to perfectly evoke the user's problem.

Create and prioritize at least one problem statement for each user type that has been defined. The problem statements are especially important to nail down because they will lead to the proposed solutions that are explained in the next section of the strategy presentation. Building consensus around the problems to be solved also helps you define what success looks like in the fourth strategic building block, *why*.

STRATEGY BUILDING BLOCK 3: WHAT

The *what* is your solution. The what is contingent on the first two strategic building blocks (the where and the who) being well understood. The solution is a high-level view of an offering, either a product or a service. As design professionals, we know the line between product and service is fast becoming blurry. A product is traditionally a physical good—an automobile, a vacuum, or a sneaker. But in today's digital world, software is also a product. A service is not physical; it's intangible. But services may include physical and digital elements. Examples of services are customer service (obviously), hospitality, or advice.

Though this section does not require any additional gathering of research, it does include a workshop. That's right; it's time to put your expert facilitation skills and creative diplomacy to the test. If you need a refresher on the basics of a workshop, reread Chapter 2, "re-Design School."

THE WORKSHOP: IDEATION

The objective of the workshop is to kickstart big thinking and generate several quality ideas that will help the core team shape a high-level conceptual solution. Remind participants that they will not be mocking up screens or assembling a prototype—that work is done in the next phase. Here, we still rely on our words and support our ideas with sketching (artisan mechanical pencils preferred, obviously).

Pre-workshop

The strategic designer knows that preparation is crucial. Your first action item in the pre-workshop process is to craft the agenda. This workshop should take place over three days:

- The first workshop day is a four-hour block dedicated to reverse-engineering the *who*.

- The second day is the gap day. Although there is no formal workshop session, the gap day asks each participant to complete homework.

- The third workshop day is the final four-hour block dedicated to iterating on the homework submissions.

Remember to avoid extending each in-person workshop day past the designated four hours. Any longer than four hours increases the likelihood of fatigue and burnout. After that point, the quality, thoughtful work will decrease.

Select and Invite Approximately 10 Participants. Now that you know exactly what the workshop is set out to accomplish, invite participants beyond the core team. This is the time to cherry-pick your most creative colleagues who always ask good questions and have a knack for envisioning unique and inspiring solutions. Be selective. Potential attendees should include anyone who will help accomplish the objectives that were agreed on. Be sure to tap innovative thinkers on other product teams that may overlap with your proposed work as well as helpful subject matter experts (SMEs) who can provide additional insights into business and user needs, analytics, and the competitive space. You may choose to also include senior stakeholders whose input may be required for approvals. But when it comes to including a senior stakeholder, be aware of the risk of unintentionally causing the other participants to censor what they contribute. Any stakeholders participating should be happy to set aside their trump card (it's their way or the highway) and roll up their sleeves. The decision-making process of whether a participant is a good choice or bad choice should apply to all potential participants. Above all, seek great collaborators; be sure to pass on the egomaniac who will suck the air out of the room. Finally, for those senior stakeholders who are a great value-add, let them know they do not need to attend for the entire duration. SMEs and senior stakeholder can often attend for an hour or so to provide input and then be sent on their way. The group should total between 10 and 12 active full-time workshop participants.

The Invite, the Ask, and Pre-workshop Materials: Carve out time to write the invite, complete with a clear expectation. You are asking all participants to come together as a larger team and collaborate to solve the problem that you've identified. Some, but not all, of the solutions that come out of the workshop will most likely go into the larger definition of your product. Attach pre-workshop materials that each participant will need to familiarize themselves with before Day 1. To keep participants focused (and to be considerate of their time), limit the pre-workshop materials to the work-in-progress strategy deck.

Secure Conference Room and Supplies: Unless your team is living large with a spacious team room, you'll need to secure a larger conference room to hold the workshop. This room should have ample whiteboards, an array of markers, and a stockpile of sticky notes. Also, before the workshop, determine which member of the core team will be the assigned notetaker. The notetaker participates but, like the facilitator, has the extra duty of capturing the many great conversations and summary of ideas for later review.

Workshop Day 1: Reverse-engineering the *who*

Day 1 is a half-day (four hours) dedicated to reverse engineering the who. This will require big thinking and hard work. Like most of us, pushing our brain power to the max taxes our energy. Here's a facilitator pro tip: always have a few baskets of energetic snacks (such as granola bars or fruit) stationed throughout the room. Productive participants are participants not disrupted by issues with blood sugar.

Review Workshop Agenda, Objectives, and Working Agreements. Review and assign owners to each action item on your agenda. Also, list the workshop's objective in the upper corner of the whiteboard for all to see. Be sure to discuss the working agreements that will carry through the next three days to keep this process positive.

Review the Company's Mission and Purpose. All of the work needs to further the company's mission and purpose. As a group, share the company's mission statement, vision statement (aspirations), and brand core values.

Review the Where and the Who. Review the strategy work thus far to ground everyone in the information that the BEDRC team has uncovered. This is the where and the who. The facilitator shouldn't be the only person standing in the front of the room and presenting the information. The business partner and researcher should also take turns presenting. Again, in the spirit of setting clear expectations, assign talking points beforehand and give everybody enough time to prepare.

How Might We Exercise. After all the background material is presented, the group begins the first of the day's two exercise activities, the How Might We (HMW) exercises. Here's how it works: The workshop facilitator prints the material from the who section and distributes copies to the group. The material in the who is a treasure trove of potential HMW questions. Start with the problem statement. Have the group take a few minutes and circle all the words that beg to be paired with an HMW. From top to bottom, talk through all the circled words. The facilitator, a pro at writing HMW questions, will frame the group's thinking into the HMW syntax, writing each HMW candidate on the board. You may find participants hesitant at first if they are new to HMW, but they should quickly get the hang of it and start to chime in to contribute their own or edit an existing HMW.

For example, "makes me feel anxious" can be turned into "How might we help alleviate the customer's anxiety?" Do this for the problem statement, empathy map, and customer journey map (**Figure 5.6**). And at the end of the exercise, always—repeat always—take a picture of the whiteboard. You never know who may accidentally erase it.

What If . . . Exercise. At this point, the group has an entire whiteboard full of HMWs. Now the task is to generate ideas against the HMW questions. This is the day's second exercise activity.

The facilitator sets the timer for 10 minutes, perhaps even setting the brainstorming mood with music (think chill hop, classical or jazz). Participants each grab a pad of sticky notes and find a comfortable spot to sit. Choose one HMW question to start with, and on a sticky note write "Finish the sentence 'What if . . . .'"

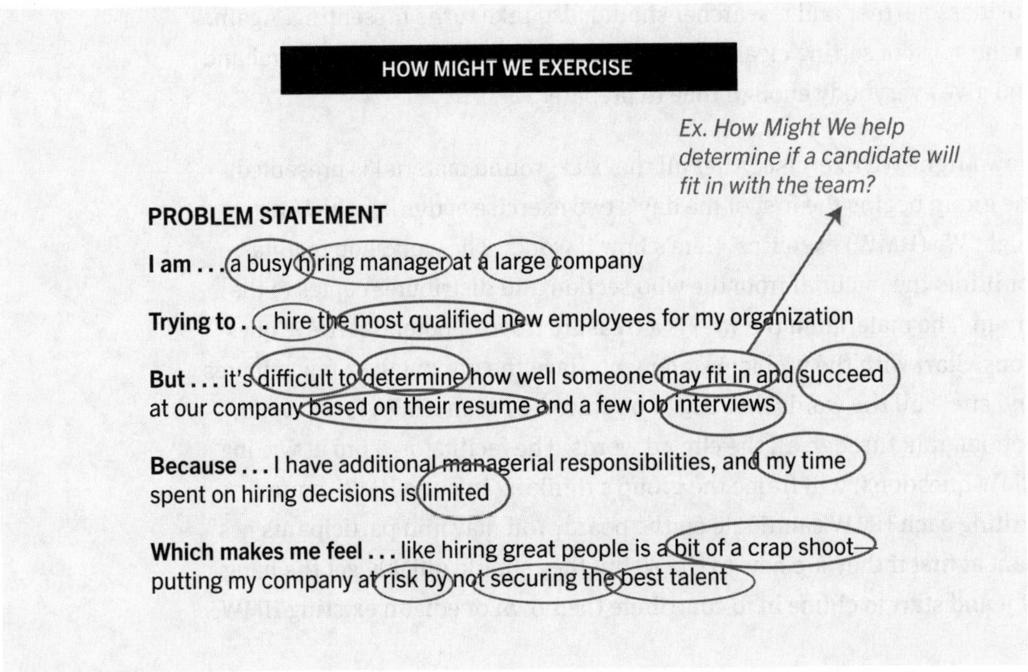

FIGURE 5.6 HMW exercise example.

For example, for the HMW question "How might we help alleviate the customer's anxiety?" one suggestion might be "What if we [the company] proactively reached out to the customer, only when necessary?" Write as many what-ifs as you can (one per sticky note). At the end of the 10 minutes, each participant gets up in front of the group to share their ideas one by one, and then hands the stickies to the facilitator. Once everyone in the has presented, the whiteboard will be a sea of ideas. Then group the stickies into themes, also called affinity mapping. A lot of the ideas will look similar and be redundant, but that's okay—those tend to be some of the strongest ideas. The group can now discuss the emerging themes. Once the group understands the themes, they are better set up for success with their homework.

Gap-day homework

Allow for a gap period in between the two sessions. This 24-to-48-hour period is just enough time to allow participants to reflect on the group brainstorming and further their own thinking.

Homework. Each participant is tasked with a homework assignment to complete on their own. The assignment is to pick one or two themes or ideas from the what if . . . list and flesh out those ideas in a storyboard fashion. If possible, the group members should coordinate with one another to make sure all the ideas are covered by someone in the group.

The facilitator should explain these instructions: Each idea is presented as a three-part storyboard using a single sheet of paper. Fold the paper in thirds. The first third on the left is the story's beginning (setting up the problem), the middle third is the middle (the proposed solution), and the final third on the right is the end (the outcome). Sketch out the idea as a concept, with the respective HMW top of mind. The completed storyboard illustrates how the proposed solution is solving the problem. Participants will bring their homework to workshop Day 2, ready to present.

Workshop Day 2: Remix

Who doesn't love a good remix? Remixing is a particularly fun workshop segment for everyone involved, but it always seems to be an especially big hit with senior stakeholders. These executives, who are often cooped up in meetings all day, far removed from actual designing, will leave positively invigorated after a day of remixing concepts.

Agenda and Objectives. The objective of Day 2 is to leave the workshop with several viable concept ideas that the core BEDRC team will refine.

Concept Presentations and Remixing. Each of the 10–12 participants take a turn presenting their homework. Each presenter tapes their storyboard page(s) to the wall, gallery style, and stands in front of the group as they talk through their idea—with the group's full attention. It's important that the group collectively respects each presenter's time. No interrupting. As audience members observe and take notes on each presentation, they should keep a scratch sheet of remixing ideas. Define a remix as a new concept that is created by modifying someone else's idea or melding concepts from multiple presenters. One concept can build on and augment another concept for the better.

Break into Teams. When homework presentations are complete, take a 20-minute break. After everyone is caffeinated, fueled, and caught up on their email and social media, divide the group into three-to-four person teams. Ask up front if there are special requests to work together; participants may want to team up based on complementary concepts. Set the timer for 30–45 minutes. Each team is now charged with fleshing out one or two detailed concepts, working with their own homework and remixing notes.

Presenting and Voting. While teams are collaborating and before anyone presents, reinforce the strategic groundwork. Remind the group who the customer is, repeat the problem statement (it should be clearly visible in your workshop space), then review the HMW questions and what if . . . themes. Time to present! Each team designates a speaker. That person tapes the new concept storyboard sketches to the wall and presents them to the group. At the end of all the team presentations, the wall should resemble a gallery of provocative and intriguing solutions. Then it's time to vote. Give each workshop participant two dot stickers. Senior stakeholders, who may now just be arriving for the final presentations, each get one gold sticker. Gold stickers carry the most weight, as you may imagine. Group members can vote for a specific element of a concept, perhaps a feature or interaction that really stood out, rather than voting for the concept as a whole. At the end of voting, the facilitator walks through the results. Ask for commentary from the group along the way. Pay special attention to the concepts that received the highest number of votes.

Wrap-up for the Day. Finish the session by striking the final objective off the whiteboard list. Success! That's a wrap. With a successful workshop behind you, your core team should have a number of conceptual solution ideas, a lengthy list of remix suggestions, and a bucket of brainstorming gems to pull from.

Beyond the fleshed out solution storyboards and sketches, even simply building a treasure trove of HMW and what if . . . sticky notes will prove priceless for your future ideation needs. This stuff is gold! Be sure to follow up with participants to express your gratitude and get their feedback on the format of the workshop.

Post-workshop

Now that the team has a mountain of material to pull from, the task at hand will be to clearly articulate the essence of the high-level solution. Do this by identifying the unique value proposition and key differentiators and by providing a broad overview of how the product works. The work may not come together in that sequential order; this is okay.

SLIDE: THE ELEVATOR PITCH

A masterful way of connecting ideas is to brainstorm analogies. Start with an analogies exercise. Remember that an analogy is simply the comparison of two seemingly unlike things based on conceptually similar attributes. It is an incredibly powerful way to convey your unique value proposition—for example, *Uber for your homework*. With the core group, this exercise will begin to craft this one-liner. Clear your focus to the big ideas that came out of the recent workshop. Generate a list of analogies that could represent the essence of the product. Talk through the list, mixing and matching analogies until you've refined the one-liner to its simplest form that encapsulates the biggest impact. Ultimately, the analogy becomes a shorthand description of the product—its internal tagline.

With the tagline in a good spot, if your product strategy proposes a new product or service, generate a list of potential names for your offering. This probably won't be the official name of the product or service. But it is important to establish a respectable hypothetical project nickname that is fitting to the effort. A project name has the power to give life to a product that doesn't exist yet. Brainstorm a list of hypothetical product names and write them on the team's whiteboard. The team can vote on the options over a week's time. The name should be relevant to the company that you are working for and should reflect the brand principles. A good mental exercise is to make a list of the words that live in the intersection of the brand and the benefits. From there, adjust for puns and play on words. The cleverer, the better. For example, in the job placement sector, a tool that matches talented people with the right job based on company culture fit could be named *Medley*.

The elevator pitch, or solution statement, comes next. It succinctly summarizes the product idea; this is no place for jargon or overly technical terms. With that in mind, the team will dedicate a few working sessions to this work. The elevator pitch may be only a brief paragraph but will require big thinking and hard work, just as the problem statement did. Follow this general format:

- You can open the elevator pitch with a question that reflects the user's primary problem. This helps create a personal connection with the audience; start with "Have you ever . . . " followed by the situation the user faces. "Have you ever been able to get an accurate sense of a job candidate's personality and working style based solely on their resume?"

- Introduce the name of your product and product category. Re-state the one-line description of the target audience and their needs as they relate to this initiative; for example, "Our product Medley is for the hiring manager who needs to efficiently & accurately assess whether a candidate may be a good fit for both a job role and the company culture."

- State the unique value proposition (UVP) or primary benefit—the reason the customer would buy this product over the competition; for example, "Our product Medley is like *Match.com* for your hiring needs."

- State the key competitive differences that clarify how this product is unlike the competitive offerings or alternatives; for example, "Other products pair potential candidates with your business needs by solely assessing their hard skills and professional history. Medley provides qualified matches based on culture fit to help companies retain good talent, longer."

Your team's goal is to create an enticing and uncomplicated statement capable of explaining the solution within the time it takes to ride an elevator, which is less than 30 seconds.

SLIDE: HOW IT WORKS

This slide speaks to how the product works. If we know the unique value proposition, using the example "Match.com for your hiring needs," then we know, at a very high level, how that offering should work. Think of it as if you're introducing someone to a new product, its features and benefits, and how it would meet their needs (solve their problems)—in a handful of steps. A good exercise is to write a marketing blurb or onboarding content that explains how the product works to a potential new user; for example, "We are going to start by doing x, then y is going to happen, and the final outcome is z, because we understand your needs." This slide ultimately illustrates, at a very high level, how the team will approach the tactical work (**Figure 5.7**).

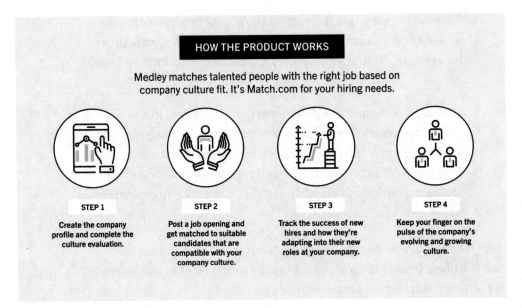

FIGURE 5.7 Example slide, "How it works."

SLIDE: IMPROVED CUSTOMER JOURNEY

This slide revisits the original customer journey map. Draft an updated version where the customer's experience is improved with the proposed solution in place. The revised customer journey will illustrate how the proposed offering provides value as compared to the current journey. It will show how you plan to alleviate the user's pain points and implement elements that will add delight to the overall experience. Note that in the next phase, this improved customer journey will be the base of the experience story.

STRATEGY BUILDING BLOCK 4: WHEN

The final strategic building block, the *when*, makes the case for timing: technological timing. Make no mistake, if the first four of our strategic building blocks come together, the time to get started is always *immediately.* There is always a way to get started *now*, with the available technology. But perhaps the *best* technology that helps create the *best* experience is still experimental (artificial intelligence) and won't be ready for primetime for another few years. Perhaps the technology that creates the best experience doesn't even exist yet and needs to be invented! The strategy must take this into account. Timing is everything, especially technological timing.

"The when" is twofold, broken into two slides: The Timing Is Now, and The Timing Is [fill-in-the-blank].

WHEN: GATHER, ANALYZE, SYNTHESIZE

This is the section that your engineering partner, the "E" of BEDRC, will lead. They'll begin by completing a thorough, candid analysis of the company's current platforms, available technology, and available resources. Don't assume the technology is all viable and in good standing; the team will need an honest assessment of how things are right now, warts and all.

After the in-house assessment, your engineering partner will gather a holistic view of the technological landscape of the sector you are in, covering everything that is used today, emerging trends, and the technology that's on the horizon (cutting-edge, leading-edge, bleeding-edge). They'll also complete a high-level engineering analysis of the hypothetical offering itself, determining the heaviest technological lifts of capabilities that could be required. Know that, among the heaviest lifts, is likely the special sauce that your company will want to develop in-house.

SLIDE: THE TIMING IS NOW

This slide sets expectations. Speak to the in-house technology that your team has at their disposal and will leverage for this project. Remember, frame this as an honest assessment. For example, perhaps the main technology stack is built on legacy code and has become increasingly unstable over the past decade. The head of development often refers to it as "a house of cards," collapsing a little bit more every time a new feature is added. Your team, and stakeholders, need to hear this to address it.

This slide also reviews additional technology needs, not currently in-house, that will need to be hired, acquired or developed to get started.

SLIDE: THE TIMING IS [. . .]

This slide is a prediction of the way the future technology landscape will evolve (as it always does) to best serve our experience. When this technology is finally available, we'll hit our stride. But not every company is a tech giant with bottomless cash flow, endless experimental resources, and time to kill. So, a clear case needs to be made to commit to longer-term investments and a solid guesstimate to when that future will be here. Include promising experimental technology and explore blue-sky inventions. Be sure to weigh both pros and cons and highlight any foreseeable challenges.

STRATEGY BUILDING BLOCK 5: WHY

This section of the strategy expresses why the proposed product will further the company's mission and purpose and will do so profitably.

WHY: GATHER, ANALYZE, SYNTHESIZE

Every company should have a mission statement that explains a crystal clear directive and underlying core philosophy. This is a company's North Star.

A company should also have an aspirational state, or vision statement (not to be confused with product vision). The company's vision is a glimpse into their future, touching on the business they want to become.

This vision serves as an opportunity evaluation framework: the business should gradually take on more customers and create offerings that serve that aspirational state.

Locate a copy of the company's mission statement. Hopefully it's not too difficult to find; it may be posted on the company's public facing website, front and center. As stated in Chapter 4, you may learn that this all-important mission (what your company does) and purpose (why they do it) are vaguely defined, unclear, or even left unaddressed. Unfortunately, this is more common than you think at many large companies. If this is the case, do your best to write up your own draft by gathering knowledge from leadership throughout the company. Know that different parties may give you conflicting information, based on their own goals and personal perspective. As you work on crafting the draft, know which parties' opinions matter and whose are heard out of consideration. For example, the CEO's opinion matters. The company's brand guidelines and principles, also known as core values, are also helpful to have on hand.

Your business partner will be responsible for the business model. As the strategic designer, you may find business models outside of your domain, but it's important that you're capable of having an intelligent conversation about business and revenue models. Here's the overall gist: You know that your company aims to earn more money than it spends, that you turn a profit. A business model is a plan for that profit. It's the economic framework that includes how your company plans to create value around an offering (a product or service) and deliver that offering to a customer to make money. For example, a popular type business model is the razor-and-blade business model—essentially give the razor away for free and make money off the blades. Another type of business model is continual revenue, or a subscription model. This model is well suited for products that have regular upgrades, such as cloud-based software. Within a sector, business models vary only slightly between the competition. Today, business model innovation—for example, fundamentally changing a product's delivery mechanism, like a subscription—is equally as valuable to a company as product innovation. What ends up happening is when one company finds success with a new, cutting edge business model, the rest of the competition in the industry will often quickly follow suit. Your business partner will exhaustively analyze what the competition is doing, taking in the breadth of options available and making recommendations for innovation. Innovation often happens by "remixing" existing models into a new model type.

Be sure to also locate the company's business objectives. Typically, a well-organized company will have clarified how high-level objectives break down across the long-term, mid-term, and short-term. If not, your business peer is responsible for compiling this list.

SLIDES: ADVANTAGES

Your business partner will have done a thorough analysis of the competitive landscape, so they've identified similar or competing products and provided a synopsis of their strengths, weaknesses, market share, customer awareness, and sentiment. Here you present why your proposed offering is superior to the competition's, highlighting your advantages. You can help support this work by lending organizational and data visualization skills.

SLIDE: NORTH STAR ALIGNMENT

This final slide makes the case *why* this product will further the company's mission, achieve business objectives, and ultimately serve the company's vision—getting the business one step closer to the company they want to become.

Your business partner will present the various business model options— the plan to deliver the proposed offering to customers to make money. This will most likely include business model projections that will illustrate the costs and expenses versus the price you can charge for the offering. In real time, stakeholders can model hypothetical factors against different delivery mechanisms that could impact positive cash flow.

With the company mission and business model recommendation top of mind, your business partner will be responsible for preparing the definition of success for your proposed offering. This can include key performance indicators (KPIs) and a measurement plan. After all, what's the point of having a goal unless you understand whether or not you've reached it?

FINAL TOUCHES

The presentation deck is nearly complete! Here are the last few final touches: the cover, table of contents, team, and appendix.

THE COVER

Make a great first impression. The cover is the team's first 30 seconds to kickstart excitement and establish a strong connection with the stakeholder audience—or anyone who comes across this "walking" deck down the road. There are a handful of pieces to the cover: the product name, the tagline, the technical line, and a background image. The technical line consists of one or two contact persons, the team name (if you have one), and the date. Dates should reflect the last time the deck was updated, rather than the date of the presentation. As with your proposal, it never hurts to add a glossy cover slathered in on-brand-flavored eye candy that will hook those viewers' attention from the start. The cover image should be clean—the core message front and center, without any clutter getting in the way. Here, clean means the image visually captures the tagline analogy, reflecting the essence of the product. The aesthetics should be modern, but not be overly trendy.

TABLE OF CONTENTS

Aside from listing the sections of the document, at the top of the table of contents (TOC), it's a good move to post the strategic building blocks blueprint statement and visual diagram of the product vision process. This sets expectations for your stakeholder audience.

THE TEAM

Don't underestimate the power of being effusive about the team's abilities. Every project is at the mercy of the expertise of a team and their professional working chemistry. A team whose core members have both high expertise and working chemistry is special. That special makeup will better overcome obstacles and will collectively raise the bar. This caliber of team is not so easy to come by. But if you can find it, most stakeholders can be persuaded to let a special team further investigate a fledgling idea that they themselves can't quite wrap their heads around yet—putting faith in the team's abilities over their own understanding of the idea.

On this slide, list names and roles of all team members and stakeholders (photos are nice if available). This may include an indication of which stakeholders should be included for any required reviews. Write a handful of bullet points on the unique attributes that qualify the individual for the BEDRC core role on the team. Include primary role responsibilities and note the individual's experience level with relevant accomplishments. Alongside each person's primary role, include their supporting secondary strength. For example, the strategic designer may also be a talented writer. Or perhaps the business partner is a former designer who transitioned careers and now makes for a killer teammate. Remind stakeholders of the quality of each individual and the caliber of the collective team every time they encounter this last slide. This credits section also serves as a reminder to team members of their own accountability and respective responsibilities.

APPENDIX

The final slide is an appendix. Remember that mountain of research that is archived on the team's intranet folder? Be sure to list each of the documents for ease of reference.

PLAN TO PIVOT

Somewhere down the road, mid-visioneering effort, the product vision may encounter a need for a pivot, or an adjustment. Such is the nature of this work. Perhaps the team set out building x, but as it turns out, testing is proving the customer doesn't necessarily want x. Time to pivot! Perhaps the opportunity space was upended by a brand-new competitor and the user expectation bar is reset. Time to pivot! When this happens, all delivery is paused while the core team returns to this strategy phase, restarting the process. All five strategic building blocks are regroomed, and then the experience story is tweaked, the prototype altered, the work validated, and the deliverable updated. Only then, with an fresh product vision, is the delivery resumed. Chapters 7 and 8 discuss handling and recovering from pivots.

NEXT STEPS

The next step is to transition out of strategy and into the experience story phase. But first, let the team recover—give it a day or two. Once the team is ready to go, it's time for a baggage check. This is a good time to reset from the laborious strategy phase, which was likely very stressful. Schedule a retrospective with the group. All baggage should be left behind, giving the team a fresh start.

CHAPTER 6

TELLING THE STORY OF THE FUTURE EXPERIENCE

Finally, you've arrived at the chapter that utilizes the full power of your creativity. In this chapter, we get down to the nuts and bolts of crafting the future state of the offering by telling the story of the experience (**Figure 6.1**). Building to this point, you assembled your team, set up your project, and survived an impressive strategy phase—now with a robust strategy deliverable under your belt.

Don't be surprised if your business peers are coming around to appreciate the greater worth of modern-era design, as well as its newest practitioner, the strategic designer (that's you). High fives all around! Design is earning that strategic seat at the table.

In this chapter, we consider the importance of support from above, delve into the art of storytelling, and finally, explain what you must do, step by step, to create the stand-alone deliverable.

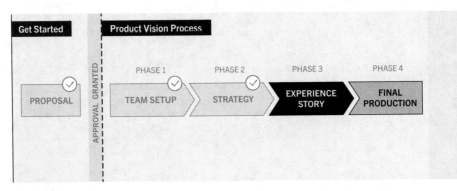

FIGURE 6.1 You Are Here.

GET SUPPORT FROM ABOVE

Heed this warning—the impulse of your business peers and product owners, after acquiring that impressive strategy deliverable, will be to skip over the rest of the product vision process to begin immediately churning out features. This is especially true for those of you employed at a feature factory—aka, a company that doesn't yet have a clear understanding or appreciation of user experience or design. So, how do you overcome this obstacle? Escalate, escalate, escalate. Escalate any and all concerns of potential product vision derailment to senior stakeholders. Remember, many of your business peers (those who haven't read this book, obviously) are coming to this effort with a gross underappreciation for what it takes to deliver a compelling and actionable product vision. Their idea of vision work is a quick, imaginative exercise that may be high on creativity and placate the design team but that doesn't add much business value. In the minds of your business peers, investing a day or two of resources to keep the designers happy (and subordinate) is worth it. However, this new approach to product vision asks that same business peer to dedicate precious time and resources for the better part of the month. So, after they hyperventilate, their primal instinct will be to shut it down. But with senior stakeholders, plus C-suite (top leadership) support, those business peers will be much more inclined to play ball.

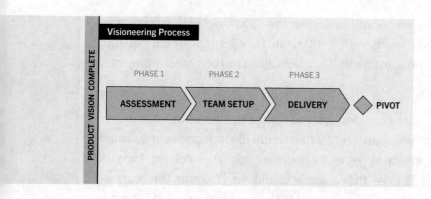

So, escalate, escalate, escalate. It's critical that you have solid support (even better, a few champions) among the executive leadership team. If you are unfortunate enough to work under leadership who is deeply resistant to change, you have a big problem on your hands. The change averse senior stakeholder is the number one red flag indicating that a product vision will be over before it even starts. Upton Sinclair, a 19th-century author and political candidate, succinctly describes why business folk can be resistant to change:

> It is difficult to get a man to understand something, when his salary depends on his not understanding it.[1] —UPTON SINCLAIR

Let's look at an example. At a financial services firm, a team successfully finishes their strategy phase and is now ready for the next phase that really digs into translating that strategy into a vision. An interesting insight that surfaced during strategy was the recent research showed most people find the topic of money to be anxiety provoking. A key study pointed out that, in a post-2008 financial crisis world, the customer is irrationally compelled to regularly log in to their online account just to

---

1 Sinclair, Upton, *I, Candidate for Governor*

see that their money is still in the account. Crazy, right? Upon confirmation that their money is indeed still there, they desperately click around for additional information that can help alleviate their stress—always to no avail.

The team suggests a case for a product vision that curbs those money-induced panic attacks—an offering that would likely decrease login activity by proactively reaching out to the customer only when needed. Even then, the aim would be to get the customer in and out. However, this particular financial services firm structures their upper-management bonuses around user engagement—specifically the number of customers logging in and executing transactions. The VP of investment offerings is incentivized to keep customers regularly logged in and actively clicking. And any clicks will do, and the more, the better. That VP understands that high click rates equal success, and in turn, an increase in success equals a higher bonus (cash that will arrive just in time for the holidays).

If a stakeholder's paycheck, and job, is dependent on doing things a certain way, they won't hear otherwise. That means your innovative product vision isn't going anywhere (but kudos for putting all that hard work into the strategy).

The lesson is, when you see these situations arise, immediately escalate to your most senior leadership. If you have it within your power, build alliances and work directly with progressive leaders who are change agents within the organization. Nevertheless, even with the power of progressive leadership behind you, your message is always the same. Repeatedly present the case for the importance of proper strategy-led product vision and why it is critical in terms of both short-term and long-term success.

Use these next two chapters to arm yourself with ironclad talking points.

FUTURE STATE

This phase creates the future state of the offering. The future state acknowledges the strategy's complex connections (the where, who, what, when, and why) by telling the story of an ideal experience and illustrating the offering's high-level features and benefits by way of a visionary conceptual solution. Throughout the story, key interactive moments convey the intentions of the product or service without getting into detailed designing. Ultimately, you're telling the story of how an aspirational product vision will forge an idealized value-based partnership between your company and your customers by meeting the needs of both the business and your target audience.

MORE THAN WORDS: A VISION

Think back to the last time you sat in on a product strategy meeting and wondered, "But what is success supposed to look like? How do we design against this?" In contrast to a dry and rudderless read-out, the product vision paints a picture of a future state that is compelling and actionable.

The product vision is the keystone that secures the bricks of our product strategy in place. It is the means we use to motivate the strategy into action.

Commit that line to memory. Only when the product strategy is complete, is the door unlocked for the team to move into the phase that crafts the future state, the story of the experience. Here we get to the meat of a product vision. The end result is a stand-alone deliverable, capable of demonstrating clear and inspirational future ambitions for a product or service without the need to add additional explanation.

A FOUR STEP PLAN

To give you a taste of what's to come, here is the high-level plan your team will work through. Unlike the strategy phase, this phase is more regimented and will keep to the sequential steps. This not only is the better path to success but is put in place to ease our stakeholders' peace of mind. Again, not many traditional businesses have faith in product vision work until they see the results and reap the benefits (i.e., think accolades or promotions). Instead of asking for blind faith, you're asking stakeholders to make an informed decision at every turn. Your plan consists of these four steps:

> Step 1: Kickoff
>
> Step 2: Storyboards
>
> Step 3: Concept Ideation and Prototype
>
> Step 4: Acceptance

Be sure not to cut corners! A thorough completion of each step is paramount to success—the team is building on the output from one step to the next. But before we dive in, you must understand how to harness strategic storytelling. Here's why: Strategic storytelling is critical to each of the four steps of this phase. Storytelling is the thread that helps teams first make sense of the product vision, and later, it will be a huge part of how you present the product vision to your stakeholders and users. So, the success of a product vision truly depends on the strength of your team's storytelling abilities.

THE ART OF STORYTELLING

Storytelling is a big part of being human. We use the timeless tradition of telling stories as a universal means of interpersonal connection, passing on essential lessons from one generation to the next, using storytelling to help us make sense of reality and the world around us. We are all storytellers. But some do it much, much better than others. Everyone has listened to a friend tell a story that has taken one too many tangents. Most of us have been cornered at the office watercooler by a well-intentioned colleague whose story drags on and on with unnecessary detail. Or perhaps *you* are that challenged storyteller . . . and you just don't know it yet (well, you're about to find out). A well-crafted story is an art form that the strategic designer looking to find success with a product vision will have to master. Thankfully, the backbone of storytelling is rooted in information design—a designer's home turf. But beyond sound structure, the key to becoming an exceptional storyteller is understanding the power of empathy.

EMPATHY

The English word *empathy* hasn't been around all that long—it was coined in the early 1900s. The contemporary usage of empathy remains a broad concept, so depending on who you ask, the definition may vary. For our purposes this definition works:

> *Empathy is the ability—and willingness—to tune into someone else's vantage point and imagine their experience through their feelings and motivations.*

Practicing empathy is best explained by the idiom "Walk a mile in another's shoes before judging them." Despite finding a place in the English dictionary only within the last century, empathy is the cornerstone of being human. Practicing empathy is the measurement of emotional intelligence.

Three types of empathy

Psychologists break empathy down into three different types:

- Cognitive empathy

- Emotional empathy

- Compassionate empathy

Cognitive empathy is the ability to identify what someone may be thinking or perceiving the feelings of others. Cognitive empathy is a skill that can be learned; the best managers are often highly tuned into their cognitive empathy abilities. Emotional empathy is the ability to vicariously share in the emotional experience of another. Just like catching a cold, we catch feelings. Compassionate empathy is the ideal—it's the balance between both cognitive (the head) and emotional (the heart) and has an actionable component that moves someone to help. Compassionate empathy leads to effective positive change in the world, large or small.

EMPATHY = STORYTELLING

Empathy isn't just a handy tool in the storyteller's toolbox; empathy is storytelling. By harnessing the power of compassionate empathy to tell a compelling story of experience, you grab the attention of your stakeholder audience and transport them to a vivid vision that allows them to live vicariously through the experience of the customer. The more emotionally charged the story, the more those empathetic hug hormones (oxytocin) flood a stakeholder's brain, deepening the bond and connection the stakeholder forms with the customer. That deep connection will move your stakeholders to take positive action. And you need your stakeholders inspired to sign off on the funding, handle nasty politics, and remove any red tape holding your initiative back from getting into market.

And that emotionally driven momentum won't stop short. Storytelling is the ultimate communication vehicle that delivers information that will absorb at a much higher retention rate than other mechanisms (think bulleted lists). Those stakeholders won't forget how they feel any time soon. Imagine, in the not-so-distant future, empathetic stakeholders who are truly tuned in to the needs of the customer and who are compelled to lead with experience rather than leading with features. Amen to that.

ADDING STRUCTURE

The way to become an exceptional storyteller is to first ground your craft in the elements that structure and shape a story. This step may seem basic, but what's the definition of a story? Simply put, a story is a series of events, fact or fiction. A plain story is just that: a time line of chronological events. The practice of storytelling seamlessly integrates all the elements to dramatically reveal why things are happening. The mistake of the amateur storyteller is to blindly feel their way through the story and haphazardly address its elements. A professional storyteller hinges their craft on mastering each and every element at their disposal. For our purposes, the fundamental elements suit your needs:

- Characters

- Story arc

- Point of view

- Theme

- Scene

- Setting

Characters. Characters are the roles that take part in the story. The key roles are the main character, the protagonist, and the antagonist. The audience experiences the story through the eyes of the main character. The protagonist is our hero and the agent who moves the plot forward. Often the main character and the protagonist are one and the same—and approaching things this way certainly makes things easier. But the master storyteller has an advanced option at their disposal: separating the main character from the protagonist, thus creating two separate entities. This makes for a more dynamic story and a move we will be optioning for the experience story. The antagonist is the villain and should be a worthy opponent to the protagonist. Lastly, secondary characters support the leading roles and, in our case, will be used sparingly.

Story Arc. The story arc, also known as a narrative arc, is the scaffolding of your plot. Most stories fall into one of a handful of story arc categories. A common story arc begins with an introduction, builds rising action to a conflict, reaches climax, enters a period of falling action, and then finds a resolution. If the protagonist and main character are one and the same, then one thread is pulled through the story arc. But if the storyteller chooses to pull the main character apart from the protagonist, two threads are pulled through the story arc. The first thread focuses on the overarching storyline and viewpoint of the central problem facing the protagonist. The second thread is that of the main characters and follows the first thread closely but tells it from a personal viewpoint.

Point of View. The point of view (POV) refers to who is telling the story and how it is being recounted. The types of POV are first person, second person, and third person. If the POV is first person, the main character is also the narrator.

Theme. The literary theme is the underlying meaning of the story and holds the important job of compelling the plot forward. Examples of common themes are love, justice, revenge, good versus evil, or coming of age.

Scene. A story is made up of scenes. A scene is essentially a mini-story that shows the characters engaging in action or dialogue. A scene should have a beginning, a middle, and an end.

Setting. The setting is all about context, describing the backdrop in which the events take place. In straightforward terms, the setting is the physical location and time period in which the story takes place.

Now that you have the basics of storytelling under your belt, you are ready to dive into the process of creating the story of the future experience.

STEP 1: KICKOFF

The kickoff may only be 60–90 minutes, but this meeting has to both motivate your team to rally past the exhaustion following the strategy phase and inspire creative greatness. Organize the meeting with the core team and stakeholders to review the plan, go over what success looks like, and importantly, get inspired. A big job of an innovative product vision is to continually spark curiosity, creativity, and inspiration in those who are executing against it. So, naturally, the people crafting it have to be inspired themselves. Need an inspirational speech?

> **TRY IT THIS WAY**
>
> Remind your team they are working on this product vision at [insert company name] because they have earned it. Getting this project successfully to this point was no easy feat. And the team will likely continue to face challenges. But now is the time to seize this exceptional opportunity and produce a product vision that is worthy of influencing high-level enterprise decisions. The possibilities are limitless on a business platform like this one—this company has plentiful cash, resources, and the brand reach to make a massive impact. So why not strive to make a massive impact and effect big change for the better? This is the opportunity not only to influence the direction of today's slated projects but to shape tomorrow's bigger picture. And the icing on the cake is we're getting paid to do it. How lucky are we?

REVIEW THE PROCESS

Start by reviewing the process with the team. This objective-oriented approach will keep the team prioritized, on task, and driving toward your deliverable. The plan also functions as a statement of work for the nervous stakeholder who needs a little more information before they have unwavering confidence in the effort. The process can be written in an email or a text document.

The Scope and Objectives. Your team will have infinitely better odds of molding a product vision that can go the distance if everyone involved understands what's expected of them and what the team should be striving to achieve at each step. Create a list of this phase's four sequential steps. Alongside each step, list a description, action items, and objective. As you learned in Chapter 2, "re-Design School," the completion of each objective is your rubric for success. The team should pace the work with a sense of urgency; the aim is to complete all the objectives within the allotted time and using the available resources. If the designated time period ends before they have completed the deliverable, the team missed the mark. At the kickoff, examine each of the four steps. It's helpful to write the plan on a whiteboard or a large sheet of paper in your team room so that it's always visible. When the team successfully completes an objective, strike it off the list.

Set Expectations. Here is the rule of thumb: Estimating Steps 1 through Step 3 is straightforward. For a well-staffed, experienced core team, dedicate at least three to five business days to each of the first three steps. The exception is Step 4, acceptance. The time and resources required at Step 4 depend on the availability of your executive team (how fast your team can get on their schedule) and the time and resources needed to design a customer study and recruit participants. Be sure to negotiate for this time at the onset of the process. All in all, communicate to stakeholders that the least amount of time an experienced team will need to get through Step 3 is approximately 15 densely packed business days—maybe 10 business days if the team is exceptionally talented and working against a tight deadline. Whatever you do, don't underestimate the amount of time it will take your team to do the work and don't skimp on resources.

A good way to condition stakeholders to the depth and time-consuming nature of this work is to use a project management and time-tracking application to scope the effort. For example, create an epic story for each of the four steps, then break down the complexity of each step into achievable stories by sizing every story against the team's resources. Again, you are talking the language that most software business stakeholders understand.

STEP 2: STORYBOARDS

This is the good stuff! In Step 2, your team will leverage their sharply tuned storytelling skills to write the experience story.

WHAT ARE EXPERIENCES?

Most designers know Don Norman as the founding father of contemporary user experience (UX). At Apple, in the 1990s he actually coined the term *user experience:*

> " The user experience encompasses all aspects of the end-user's interaction with the company, its services, and its products.[2] "

This definition may sound basic, but really, what does it mean? Any experience is someone's observation of their feelings about an encounter or occurrence. In the context of this work, a company should always be striving for their customers to observe positive feelings after an encounter with their product and service. Whether the feeling of delight comes after a surprisingly quick task within the app or an extremely helpful customer

---

2 www.nngroup.com/articles/definition-user-experience

service call, those positive feelings then influence the feelings the customer has toward the brand. This story deliverable expresses this idealized state: presenting a future experience where the user is observing positive feelings about both the product/service and the brand.

FOUR PILLARS FOUNDATIONAL TO A GREAT EXPERIENCE

After decades of analyzing, designing, delivering, using, and gathering feedback on hundreds of products and services enjoyed by millions of users, we've identified that the best ones have something in common—four things, actually. The most effective experiences are built on four universal pillars that constitute the base of how a satisfying and valuable user experience is formed. Each pillar is fairly elementary in terms of its definition, and they can be applied to any product or service in order to improve the overall customer journey (**Figure 6.2**).

Pillar 1 is Understand Customer Needs. This pillar is the obvious first and most critical step of any quality product or service and a core value of human-centered design. Fortunately, at this point your team has covered this topic extensively in the *who* portion of your product strategy phase. If you and your stakeholders don't yet possess a solid understanding of your customer and their needs, it's time to go back and revisit that product strategy presentation. Again, how your team decides to collect information about your customers is up to you. Perhaps it's all done through primary research. Maybe you decide to continually gather detailed analytics about how users interact with your product. You potentially have a user base who is willing to consistently share information about their needs with you through surveys and tools that you provide. Any way you slice it, it's imperative to keep your finger on the pulse of your users and their ever-evolving needs.

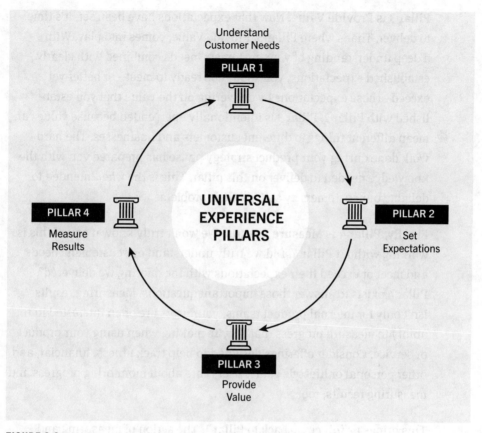

FIGURE 6.2 Universal experience pillars.

Pillar 2 is Set Expectations. You may have noticed that users tend to have increased confidence and better outcomes when expectations are made clear. This is the reason so much effort is made to optimize and enhance user onboarding activities—often when most expectation setting occurs. When users understand the capabilities of a product or service, how to make the best use of it, and what (if anything) is required on their part, it reduces the amount of anxiety they may experience during their interaction. Consider how well you're setting user expectations with your current product and service offerings. Is there room for improvement? How might you improve on this pillar with your product vision?

Pillar 3 is Provide Value. Now that expectations have been set, it's time to deliver. That's where Pillar 3, Provide Value, comes into play. With a deep understanding of your customers' needs combined with clearly established expectations, you should be ready to meet—or better yet exceed—those expectations by delivering on the value that you established with Pillar 2. Pillar 3 is intentionally open ended because value can mean different things to different customers and businesses. The hard work done during your product strategy phase has prepared you with the knowledge needed to deliver on this pillar. This is the *what* intended to delight your customers by solving their problems.

Finally, Pillar 4 is Measure Results. We won't truly know if any of this is working without Pillar 4. Did we truly understand our customers' needs and meet or exceed their expectations with the offering we delivered? Pillar 4 exists to answer those important questions. Measuring results isn't only for internal product teams; your users are often interested in the ability to measure progress that they're making when using your product or service. Consider offerings designed to help track fitness, financial, and other personal or lifestyle goals. Users care about monitoring progress and measuring results, too.

This brings us full circle back to Pillar 1. The action of measuring and analyzing results can often influence your team's understanding of your customers and can cause a domino effect—coloring how you approach the execution of each pillar moving forward. High-performing agile teams will understand and excel at this kind of iterative process and strive to continue measuring, learning, and improving the value of their offering with each iteration.

Given the universality of the pillars, your team can use them as a framework for crafting the primary scenes in your experience story. How your team defines and activates the specific details of each pillar is up to you and will set your product vision apart from competitive offerings.

THE FRAMEWORK

Thankfully, the backbone of storytelling is rooted in information design, your home turf. The structure of the experience story is a customized framework that maps the essential storytelling elements to your strategy.

Characters. The experience story's key characters are the main character, the protagonist, and the antagonist (**Figure 6.3**). As stated earlier, the main character and protagonist are often one and the same. But for our purposes, the main character and protagonist are two separate entities. The main character is the customer (the *who* building block in our product strategy). The main character should be introduced with just enough background so that the audience can identify with this person. Detailed descriptions should focus on the wants, needs, feelings, and personality traits of the character rather than physical attributes (you should already have this information cataloged as part of an empathy map created during the strategy phase). The protagonist is your company and brand. Your proposed solution (the *what* from your strategy) isn't a character per se but is instead a tool that the protagonist will use to help achieve an end goal. Think of the story of King Arthur and Excalibur. King Arthur is the protagonist. He uses his magical sword, Excalibur, as a means to defeat his

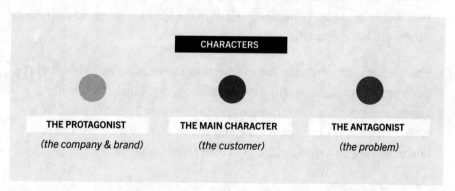

FIGURE 6.3 Visualize each participant in the story as having a role in the narrative.

enemies. In your case, the main character is the customer. The protagonist is your company, the knight in shining armor. The offering, the product or service, is Excalibur. The company may wield Excalibur or give the sword to the customer so that they can wield the power themselves. Lastly, you need an antagonist, your villain. In some experience stories, the antagonist will be an actual person, but in others, the antagonist will be a theoretical problem. For example, in software security, the antagonists are actually people with bad intentions—hackers who are trying to corrupt systems, steal data, or hold it hostage. But in financial services, the antagonist is more of a concept rather than a person. Conceptual examples could include the need for remote team members to collaborate from different locations, a lack of time, a lack of confidence in one's abilities, or overcoming anxiety (Figure 6.3).

Point of View. The experience story is told through a narrator (third person, omniscient), supplemented with the main character (first person). Third-person omniscient is told using he/she/they and has full access to the thoughts and feelings of the main character. Occasionally, you hear directly from the main character, who tells the audience about their problems, how they feel about their problems, how they discovered the solution, and what it was like when they first experienced the solution. Your audience is able to put themselves in the shoes of the main character, which will build empathy.

Theme. For your purposes, the overarching theme of an experience story (for a product or service) will likely weave together knight in shining armor, perseverance, and triumph. Your customers' lives are filled with difficult moments or problems, big and small, that must be overcome. Customers are on a quest to triumph over those problems.

Setting. The setting is all about context, describing the backdrop in which the events take place. Here, the setting describes where your customer is encountering the problem and finding the solution. The setting reflects the customers' everyday lives or an event that prompts the need for an offering. This expresses not only the physical location and time period in which the story takes place, but also the opportunity space, the *where* of your strategy.

Scenes. The scenes are reflective of the universal experience pillars (Figure 6.2). In our example there are six scenes columns (see **Figure 6.4**). The four experience pillars are flanked on each side by an on-ramp and a conclusion. The on-ramp is the first column, addressing customer awareness and product onboarding: your customer has a problem to be solved and you make them aware of a new product that could fill that void. The four middle columns each represent an experience pillar, illustrating the customer's experience with your offering: Pillar 1 is understand your customer's needs, Pillar 2 is set expectations, Pillar 3 is provide value, and Pillar 4 is measure results. The final scene is the story's conclusion: now the customer's needs are met (for now) and life continues. Writing a complementary "How Might We" (HMW) for each scene will help the team create a cohesive story.

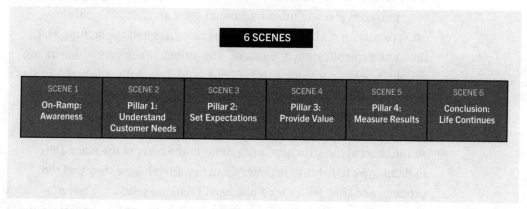

FIGURE 6.4 The six scenes of an experience story.

For example, these HMWs will work for a number of industry sectors:

> **Scene 1, On-Ramp:** How might we build awareness and educate potential customers about how your product will deliver value and solve their problem?

> **Scene 2, Pillar 1:** How might we build a deep understanding, capture, and assess your customers' needs on an ongoing basis?

> **Scene 3, Pillar 2:** How might we help customers understand your product/service so that they can get the most out of what it has to offer?

> **Scene 4, Pillar 3:** How might we use the information that you've collected about your customers to meet their needs and provide a superior experience?

> **Scene 5, Pillar 4:** How might we measure the amount of value that you've delivered to your customers?

> **Scene 6, Conclusion:** How might we see this product growing with the customer and advancing with technology?

Story Arc. The story arc is the scaffolding for your plot (**Figure 6.5**). For your purposes you will use a traditional story arc. A traditional story arc typically opens by introducing the characters and the setting, and then has a complication or incident. The problem then gets worse (rising action); reaches a turning point (climax) and, hopefully, the problem gets better (falling action); and ultimately, the problem is resolved. Your team will build the story's content against the flow of the story arc.

At the heart of the structure is the content, the body of the story. Here, in detail, you tell of the customer's journey, first, before they find the product, and then with the company, via the new product. The problem statement pulled from beginning to end, at the end, the problem is addressed, if not solved.

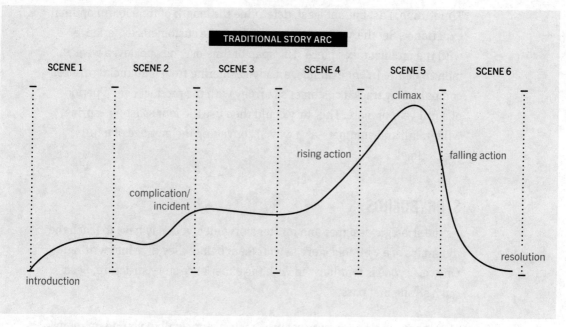

FIGURE 6.5 Traditional story arc.

The body is broken down against the story arc into six scenes. Now, if your protagonist and main character were one and the same, then one storyline thread would be pulled through the story arc. But because the main character was pulled apart from the protagonist, two storyline threads are pulled through the story arc. The overarching big thread focuses on the viewpoint of the central problem facing the protagonist (the problem that the company enlists the product to solve). Perhaps the narrator begins the story by introducing the opportunity that surfaced and the series of steps that led to discovering the customer. The story could then segue to introduce the main character. The main character's thread follows the big thread but tells it from a personal viewpoint. At the end of the last scene, the problem is solved, and a transformation has taken place.

Keep in mind that you can use your company's brand values to tailor the tone of the story. For example, an athletic sports apparel company whose core value is fun could incorporate a playful tone.

Timeframe. Last but not least, determine the length of time for an optimal experience. Set the span of time over which the customer's experience with the product takes place. The span of time may be one day, a week, a month, or a year. For example, an advice offering from a financial services company may track a customer's journey with the product over a period of a full year or more. The story could then use the four seasons—spring, winter, fall and summer—as a way of conveying the passage of a full year's time.

STORYBOARDS

As the strategic designer and master storyteller, you may have to teach the dynamics of a well-told story to your team before they dive into writing. Once everyone is familiarized with the experience story structure, flesh out a strong first pass.

Here's how to get your team set up. Create a story wall in your team room; see **Figure 6.6**. Find painter's blue tape and large index cards. With the painter's tape, make a six-column grid, each column a foot in width. Each column is a scene. Use an index card as a thumbnail (**Figure 6.7**). The left side of the index card is an illustration, and the right side is a written description. Above each column, write the scene's respective pillar and HMW question. It can also be helpful to have the story arc and a time line on the wall, a helpful reminder as you work. As you create this draft, identify the thumbnails that should show the user interacting with the actual product. Use star stickers.

Use the revised customer journey to start. Adapt the revised journey to flow with the scenes (pillars) and story arc.

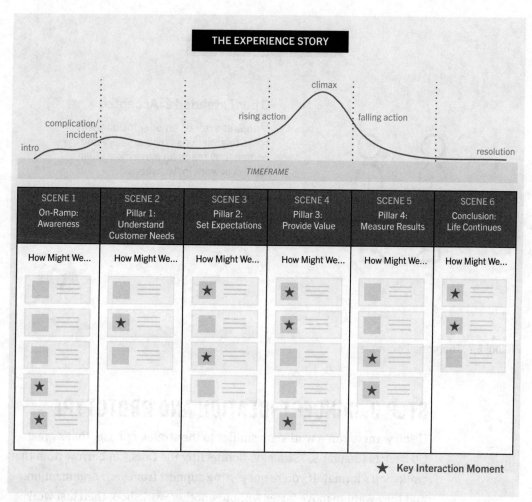

FIGURE 6.6 The team room's story wall.

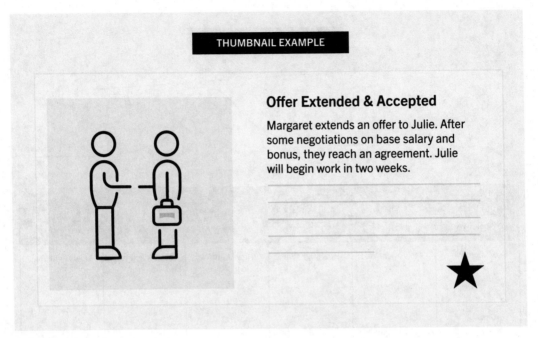

THUMBNAIL EXAMPLE

Offer Extended & Accepted

Margaret extends an offer to Julie. After some negotiations on base salary and bonus, they reach an agreement. Julie will begin work in two weeks.

FIGURE 6.7 Thumbnail example.

STEP 3: CONCEPT IDEATION AND PROTOTYPE

If you want to run a workshop similar to the strategy phase, that's great. Go back to Chapter 5, "Strategy: Connecting the Dots," to borrow from that workshop's format. If you're not getting support from your organization, and they want to move faster without another workshop, then just work with your core team. Thankfully, your core team has several conceptual solution ideas to build off of. They should also have a treasure trove of HMW and what if . . . sticky notes from that strategy workshop that will prove priceless now.

Set up daily working sessions. At the first session, quickly review the strategy deck, section by section, to ground everyone in the same information. At this point, there should be no surprises, and everyone should be on the same page. Review the experience story with the group. If needed, revisit how the story came together. That may mean talking through the experience principles and the two customer journey maps, both the original and the revised.

IDEATION EXERCISE

Here's an ideation exercise to help your core team get the wheels turning. Draw a six-column grid on the whiteboard. At the top of each column, write the scene title and respective HMW question.

With the new experience story top of mind, work to ideate conceptual ideas—features, capabilities, or initiatives—against each scene's HMW. This is a group effort. Start with the first column, "Enticing value." This column is the scene that represents the customer's first time with the product and is an onboarding phase. How might you entice the customer to use this product for the job? Perhaps a chatbot or a proactive text messaging feature reaches out to the customer. List your concept ideas. Go through this same exercise for each column scene (**Figure 6.8**).

As the team offers ideas, be on guard to call out and challenge legacy thinking—you don't want any stale ideas shaping your product vision. But always do this respectfully.

SKETCHING EXERCISE

This sketching exercise asks each team member to pick one or two ideas from the previous ideation list and flesh out those ideas in a storyboard fashion. The instructions are the same from the workshop: on a single page of paper, fold the paper in thirds. The first third is the storyboard's beginning, the second third is the middle, and the final third is the end. The complete storyboard illustrates how the proposed concept is solving the customer's problem.

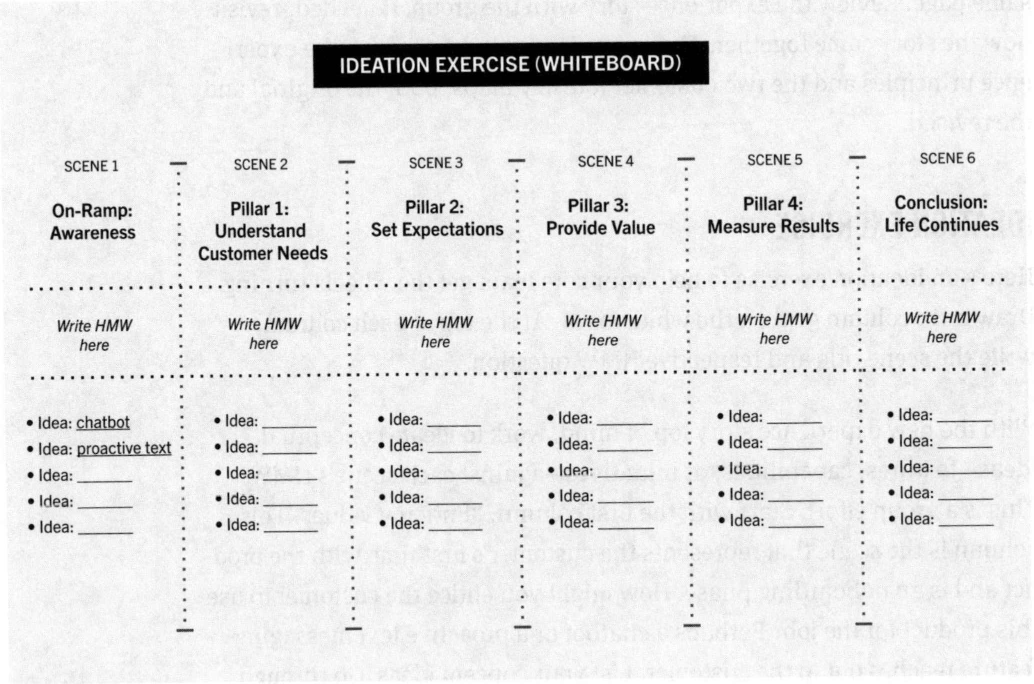

IDEATION EXERCISE (WHITEBOARD)

SCENE 1	SCENE 2	SCENE 3	SCENE 4	SCENE 5	SCENE 6
On-Ramp: Awareness	**Pillar 1: Understand Customer Needs**	**Pillar 2: Set Expectations**	**Pillar 3: Provide Value**	**Pillar 4: Measure Results**	**Conclusion: Life Continues**
Write HMW here	*Write HMW here*	*Write HMW here*	*Write HMW here*	*Write HMW here*	*Write HMW here*
• Idea: <u>chatbot</u> • Idea: <u>proactive text</u> • Idea: _____ • Idea: _____ • Idea: _____	• Idea: _____ • Idea: _____ • Idea: _____ • Idea: _____ • Idea: _____	• Idea: _____ • Idea: _____ • Idea: _____ • Idea: _____ • Idea: _____	• Idea: _____ • Idea: _____ • Idea: _____ • Idea: _____ • Idea: _____	• Idea: _____ • Idea: _____ • Idea: _____ • Idea: _____ • Idea: _____	• Idea: _____ • Idea: _____ • Idea: _____ • Idea: _____ • Idea: _____

FIGURE 6.8 A group-thinking exercise collects ideas.

REMIX EXERCISE

It's always time for a remix! Who doesn't love remixing? If you need a thorough refresher, revisit this segment from the strategy workshop from Chapter 5. In short, each team member tapes their sketching exercise to the wall, gallery style, and stands in front of the team as they talk through their idea—with the group's full attention. The group takes notes of *remixing* ideas. Remember, a remix is defined as a new concept that is created by modifying someone else's idea or melding multiple concepts from various presenters. One concept can build on and/or augment another concept for the better. After each sketch is presented, the group works together again. The team is now charged with fleshing out a handful of detailed concepts, working from all the sketches and remixing notes.

Coming out of the working sessions, the team should have a clear idea of how to assemble the conceptual solution—and have ample storyline ideas. Now you're prepared to both finalize the experience story and define the conceptual solution, and from it, craft a basic prototype. The team can divide these responsibilities to work simultaneously and in sync.

FINALIZE THE STORYBOARDS

If several variations to the main storyline came out of the working sessions, the team should identify the variation to move forward with. Then, polish each scene into sketched thumbnails—quickly done, small drawings that help your ideas take shape. Remember that each scene is a mini-story. By using the index cards and story wall, you can easily move the thumbnails around.

Once your team has decided on the story flow, storyline, and scene breakdown, the content strategist will smooth out the work. The team's content strategist, or the team member with strongest writing chops, should be partnering with the designer—the designer sketches, the content strategist writes. Remind the writer that they aren't crafting a scripted dialogue here. If dialogue is required in the next phase, that's where that task is executed.

As you work through the storyboards, highlight one or two thumbnails in each scene where it would be helpful to show a prototype screen.

CRAFT A BASIC PROTOTYPE

Now is the time to shape the conceptual solution into a simple prototype form. But before your technologists and developers get too excited, remind them what a prototype is. A prototype is a testable, early-stage release of a product, service, or process that you want to build. For this purpose, your prototype will take its most basic form: screens that correlate to the experience pillars and demonstrate, at a high level, how the user will interact with the product. We're not talking about a fully functioning, high-fidelity software build. Overengineering a prototype by adding too much unnecessary detail is often the biggest mistake a team can make. The longer a team spends refining and perfecting a prototype, the more attached to it they'll become. This makes people less inclined to make adjustments based on feedback. The team should be able to pivot against the prototype work with only a few days of tactical work lost. A team who is investing weeks or months nurturing a prototype build has taken the work way too far—this type of build is often called a "prototype baby"—and will pay for it sooner rather than later. For the product vision, craft the prototype by identifying only the most critical screens and interactions that help you tell the experience story.

Quick note: When a vision is set to the near or mid-term, you will notice that creating the simple prototype is more straightforward because you have a better understanding of the technological capabilities. But if the vision is intended for a more distant future, the prototype can be a mind-bending challenge simply because you have very little frame of reference. But who doesn't love a challenge?

STEP 4: ACCEPTANCE

That was a lot of work! Make sure you and your team are taking time to celebrate small discoveries and wins along the way, and take a deep, cleansing breath before jumping into the next step, acceptance.

Of course, transparency has been a primary theme during this entire process; you've brought your critical stakeholders along for the ride through every step of your product strategy and vision odyssey. Frankly, if you've been waiting to share your progress, how very "waterfall" of you— things are probably about to get messy. During this process you've built in opportunities to share the work and collect incremental feedback from customers as well as executive leadership. The acceptance step is the last gut check prior to producing the final deliverable that will express your product vision to the organization. By now you have everything you need to share your proposed direction with your boss's boss's boss and representatives of your target audience (strategy, customer journey, elevator pitch, storyboards, prototype, etc.).

These are some questions you want answered:

- How do you know with a high degree of confidence that the product vision you and your team have put together is worthwhile?

- Is the vision transformative?

- Is it achievable?

- Will it really make a difference in the lives of your customers and help the business achieve or exceed its goals?

In terms of getting feedback from users, work with your research partner to design a study with your target audience that will allow them to provide candid feedback on the concepts your team has created. This isn't a usability test, and it may take some additional effort to recruit participants who are on the creative side and capable of evaluating conceptual material. Share the elevator pitch, how the proposed solution could solve their problems and deliver value through the journey map, and provide any prototypes or proofs of concept that have been built. When you hear comments like "How soon can I get this?" you'll know you're on the right track.

Work with your business partner and senior stakeholders to get time on the calendar with the executive team. You'll probably be nervous to share what you've put together, but you've got this! And you definitely want the C-suite to have your back when it's time to share the final product vision broadly within the organization. Remember, if the work you and your team have done makes senior executives nervous, you're most likely on the right track. Change is hard. Big ideas and transformational change often make people uncomfortable. If it was easy, anyone could do it.

Any comments and critiques from the acceptance period should be considered honestly. As a team, it's up to you to determine what final changes need to be made before commencing with the last phase of a product vision: production.

THE LAST PRODUCT VISION PHASE: FINAL PRODUCTION

This is where all the pieces come together into its final form (**Figure 6.9**). The product vision deliverable merges the story of the experience and the conceptual solution into a single stand-alone vehicle. What does stand-alone mean? It should be able to speak for itself, without the need for team members to include additional clarification.

DETERMINE LEVEL OF EFFORT

At this point, the team has everything they need for production. Now you ask your stakeholders which deliverable effort level they want to move forward with. Producing the final stand-alone deliverable will require one of three levels of effort depending on your available time, resources, and the level of impact you'd like the vision to deliver: a lighter lift, medium lift, or heavy lift.

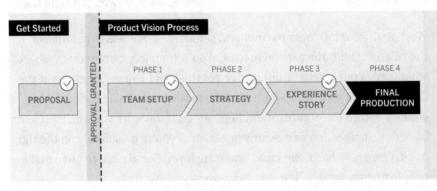

FIGURE 6.9 You Are Here, final production.

Light lift

The light effort is the minimum amount of work—and time—the team will be tasked with. The most straightforward option is to use presentation software like Microsoft PowerPoint or Apple Keynote to build the story of the experience slide by slide.

Each scene gets a section with multiple slides. Each slide is a thumbnail of the storyboard: supporting dialogue or content, a sketch drawing depicting what's going on in the thumbnail, and the conceptual solution screen. Be sure to timebox the sketching. It's important to keep to sketching and avoid getting sucked into polished drawing. Those who can illustrate know the difference—it's a huge amount of time.

Another viable option to present your team's product vision is to design and build a simple marketing landing page or microsite. Imagine that you're marketing a real product to your target audience. When building the page, consider how you might describe the features and benefits of the product or service, demonstrate how users will interact with it, and clearly illustrate the value that it provides. You may also consider including pricing options to illustrate the potential business model. An added bonus of this approach is that the landing page is tailor-made for your target audience and can be shared with them to collect feedback and validate the

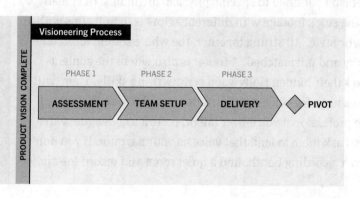

direction of your team's work. The more content and functionality you add to a microsite or landing page, the more it can transition into a medium level of effort.

Medium lift

A medium effort takes those options further—think higher-fidelity storyboards, detailed comic book panels, and additional features and content on a landing page. Perhaps the sketching evolves into more detailed drawings to bring the story to life. There are bound to be artists in your design program, some even semi-professional. Digital illustrated work and short video demos could also add motion and interactivity.

Heavy lift

The heaviest effort can be quite a production but, when pulled off, is incredibly impressive, not to mention inspiring. The option here is singular: think movie trailer, complete with video footage and production editors. The trailer is a 3–4-minute realization of the storyboards. If you don't have the budget to hire a professional video production crew—complete with lighting, audio, location scouts, and actors—you can use stock video footage. Concerned that stock footage won't seamlessly string together your narrative, given that each clip may include a different actor? The actors across the stock footage need not be the same individual. Your customer isn't confined to specific physical attributes. Get creative. The key to using stock footage with different actors is to find clips with a similar aesthetic style. All strung together, the whole should look cohesive, not clunky and mismatched. A trailer is also where the content strategist flexes their hidden Hollywood scriptwriting skills. There will most likely be a need for voice-over narration, maybe even dialogue. If you can't hire professional voice-over talent, recruit a colleague with a great voice and ask them to lend that voice as your narrator. If you don't have access to a recording booth, find a quiet room and record the audio with a smartphone. (Bonus points for buying a decent microphone that can plug into your phone and record the best possible sound.) The key resource for a trailer production will be a video editor who can seamlessly string together all the footage, animated conceptual solution screens, and voice-overs. If you can't afford to hire a professional editor, you may have access to editing software on your laptop or mobile device that will do an admirable job.

DECIDE ON EFFORT LEVEL WITH STAKEHOLDERS

How to advise stakeholders which type of deliverable to choose over another? First, consider the time period this vision takes place. Does the vision take place in the relatively near term or far off in the future? A product vision that is near-term will have a goal of achieving the vision within six months to a few years. Near-term visions are well suited for the light to medium effort. If the vision is set further in the future, then your deliverable is usually best produced as a video. Remember Apple's futuristic tablet experience video? That vision was created in the 1980s and stood the test of time before the Apple iPad and FaceTime became reality in 2011. The video format is able to display and communicate aspects that may be more nuanced and difficult to express with storyboards alone. Of course, a video will require extra resources, time, and budget, but well-produced videos are more likely to create an emotional connection with the audience.

Discuss the pros and cons of various deliverable options with stakeholders, negotiate the amount of time needed, and if required, include additional resources. For example, a lighter deliverable effort, such as a marketing landing page, would typically take an experienced team with all of the background information and supporting content at their disposal less than a week to complete. But a heavier effort, like a professionally produced video, will take longer to deliver. The postproduction work alone could easily devour two to four weeks.

POST TO AN INTERNAL AUDIENCE

The final action is to post the entire effort—the stand-alone deliverable and strategy—to your company's most widely used collaboration tool. Doing so ensures that your story is being countlessly retold with the same integrity as if the team were there to give it a voice.

Perhaps this means asking the developers to create an internal-facing (secure) URL like productvision.company.com. The page layout is made of roughly seven stacked sections. The topmost slim section of the page gives the reader a bit of context about the project and the team. Immediately following should be five sections, each dedicated to a building block: the who, where, what, when, and why. The final section is the embedded stand-alone deliverable: the video, an animation short, or a marketing slideshow. The footer provides links to email the team's primary contacts and to download the full strategy, and even directs to the small mountain of supporting documentation. You're giving the audience the opportunity to dive in as deep as they want to. This section also helps facilitate intelligent, informed conversations.

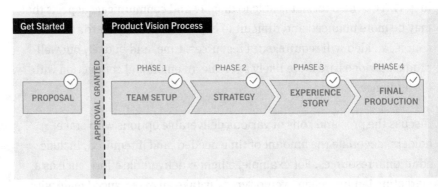

FIGURE 6.10 Product vision, complete.

PRODUCT VISION COMPLETE!

Well done! You've completed a proper strategy-led product vision (**Figure 6.10**). That opens the gate to move into the process that executes the product vision (and third part of the book), "Visioneering."

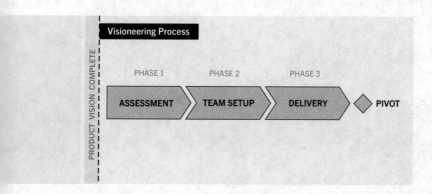

PART III
VISIONEERING

As a strategic designer, you become the co-captain of each Visioneering expedition. In Part III, discover how to activate Visioneering to be the compass pointing toward the product's promised future state while keeping it bound to the need of your business.

- Learn the approach that guides teams toward the measurable implementation of a product vision.

- Translate your bold strategy and vision into timely, actionable deliverables.

- Influence business direction to shape real-world change.

CHAPTER 7

SETTING YOUR COMPASS TO THE NORTH STAR

Congratulations on successfully leading your product vision team to cross the threshold into Visioneering. Our work up to now has focused on developing a strategy-led product vision, preparing the team for what lies ahead. Pulling it all together, **Figure 7.1** shows a high-level overview of the lengths we've gone to and goals we've accomplished to finally arrive at this point.

Way back in Chapter 4, "Getting Started with the A-Team," you asked senior leadership to sign off on the vision proposal. This green light came complete with funding, dedicated resources, and executive support. That chapter illustrated a useful format for the proposal, but really, the particular format is less important. The goal was to get leadership to sign off on the body of work, which can be achieved in any way that inspires trust, creates excitement, and motivates the people in charge to give the green light. With a green light, you moved into the product vision process, which spans four phases. In Phase 1, you assembled your team and set up the project. In Phase 2, you clarified the strategy: the who, where, what, when, and why. Once the strategy was fleshed out, your team moved into

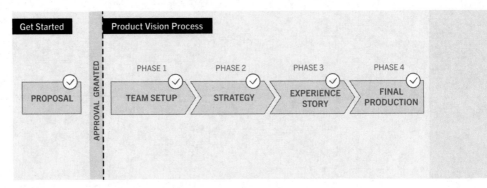

FIGURE 7.1 You are here, the first phase of Visioneering.

Phase 3, crafting the future state of the offering, by telling the story of the experience. The future state explained the strategy's complex connections (the where, who, what, when, and why) by telling the story of an ideal experience and illustrating the offering's high-level features and benefits by way of a visionary conceptual solution. By highlighting key interactive moments, you conveyed the intentions of the product or service without getting into detailed designing. Ultimately, you told the story of how an aspirational product vision will forge an idealized value-based partnership between the company and their customers by meeting the needs of both the business and the target audience. Once validated by both executive stakeholders and the customer, the team wrapped it all up into a stand-alone deliverable.

In this chapter, you officially move into Visioneering. The term *Visioneering* is a portmanteau in that it blends two words: vision + engineering. The Visioneering process translates all of the innovative thinking of a product vision into tangible output. But how exactly do teams do that? It's fair to say that this is where most product development programs get tripped up. Because most product development programs are not only heading into the delivery phase without a vision, they're working against a product *roadmap*. We hate to be the bearer of bad news, but product roadmaps are obsolete—it's time to retire them. Here's why: today every product or service journey is an uncharted expedition. Now more than ever, the landscape is unpredictable—quick to change due to the fast-paced nature

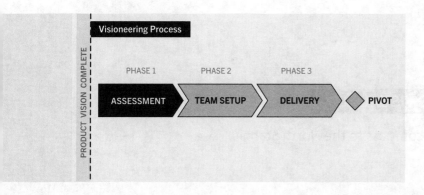

of technology and the ever-rising bar of user expectation. What the team sees in front of them today may soon shift. With this knowledge, your team knows better than to begin delivering output against a visionless, twelve to eighteen-month roadmap of features. That would inevitably lead a team to months of uninspired mediocrity or, at worst, failure. So, to navigate the terrain your team must set off on a product expedition not only with a robust strategy-led product vision, but also with a trusty compass and a clear view of their North Star. The Visioneering process is the team's compass. The North Star is their company's mission and purpose. The Visioneering process becomes the navigational tool that you will use to realize the product vision while staying aligned with the North Star every step of the way. See process visualized in **Figure 7.2** on pages 182–183.

Know that from here on out, the work will still be challenging (obviously the best kind of challenging!) but less strategic and more tactical—delivery-focused—so it will feel familiar. The team will find success by carving off thin slices of the product vision—taking an equal share of both the experience story and a bite of the conceptual solution. That slice is interpreted into tangible designs that are quickly prototyped, tested, and refined before being committed as a piece of the product or service in market. The product moves forward, bound to purposeful direction, as the team iteratively and continuously delivers an experience that is delivering on the values of the company to best serve the customer. So, with that, pack your expedition bags—it's time to venture off.

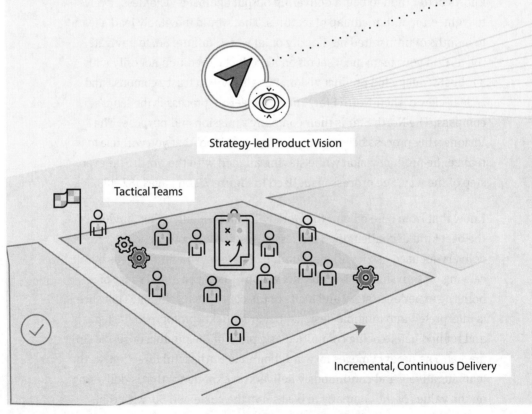

VISIONEERING VISUALIZED

Setting your compass to the North Star

Strategy-led Product Vision

Tactical Teams

Incremental, Continuous Delivery

FIGURE 7.2 The Visioneering process visualized.

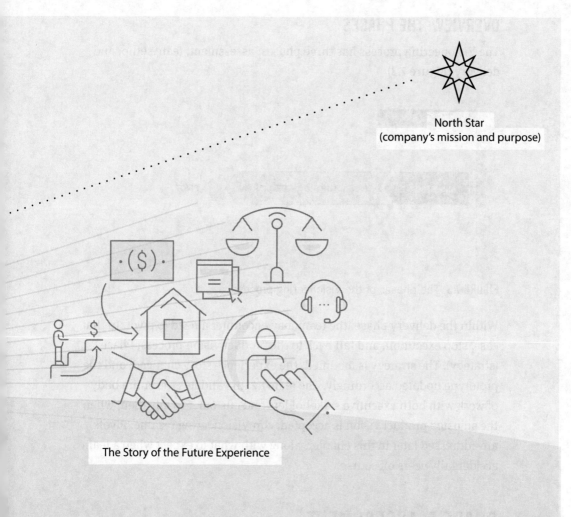

North Star
(company's mission and purpose)

The Story of the Future Experience

OVERVIEW: THE PHASES

The Visioneering process has three phases: assessment, team setup, and delivery (**Figure 7.3**).

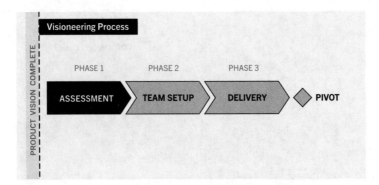

FIGURE 7.3 The phases of the Visioneering process.

Within the delivery phase, the team may encounter a need to pivot. In that case, stop execution, and fall back to the product vision process, Phase 2 (strategy). The strategy is modified, the experience story changed, and the prototype updated accordingly. The team again validates the entire body of work with both executive stakeholders and customers. Only then, when the adjusted product vision is accepted, can Visioneering resume. Pivots are addressed later in this chapter, along with what to expect when a team accidentally veers off course.

PHASE 1: ASSESSMENT

This first phase of Visioneering is an up-front assessment that will help your team identify what tactical work needs to be done, what it will take to do that work, and how to staff against it. We will do this by cataloging: initiatives, actions and resources (**Figure 7.4**).

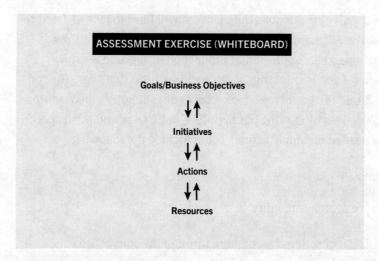

FIGURE 7.4 Assessment exercise.

You, the strategic designer, and your business partner can do the necessary prep work prior to gathering the rest of the BEDRC team and stakeholders. First, review the strategy's product goals and business objectives. Any and all work the team identifies should roll up to these. For example, a common business objective in the digital age could be:

> Reduce the amount of money we're spending on customer service call centers.

The strategic initiatives roll up to that objective and answer how we are going to accomplish that objective. Example initiatives could include the following:

> Digital transformation of all services to increase the customer's ability to both get personalized information and act on that information without needing to speak to a customer service representative.

Then, write out all of the *actions* the business will have to take to deliver on the initiatives. Examples of actions are services, product features, marketing campaigns, supplemental product offerings, and technical infrastructure. If you're thinking, didn't we already do that? Yes. The conceptual solution—the prototype—took a best guess at how to answer the strategy's objectives by carving out high-level initiatives and the respective actions needed. Example actions could include the following:

- Chatbot

- Improve search capability

Complete this list of actions by combing through the storyboards and conceptual solution and writing all actions on the whiteboard.

EXERCISE: MAPPING ACTIONS TO RESOURCES

Now your team's task is to break down the list of actions into meaningful work. Organize a working session with the core team and stakeholders. A decent working session should take a couple of hours to identify and divvy up the work.

First step always is to review the product vision, the experience story and big themes. You can reference the storyboard wall or, for the sake of readability (for those who are nearsighted), provide a copy of the storyboards to each working session participant. Then talk through the product goals and initiatives and review the list of actions—the actions should be written on the whiteboard in a grid of six columns, the list of actions correlating to each scene.

Now you will take it one step further. With all the actions identified, go through the exercise of assessing the resources the team needs to execute those actions. Resources are talent & skills (people), design assets, or technology assets. Examples of design assets are brand guidelines, a design system, a visual language, or tone-of-voice guidelines. Examples of technology assets include CRM, marketing automation, and content management systems, artificial intelligence engines, databases, or search algorithms.

Let's use the chatbot as an example. The chatbot is the action. Possible resources to execute the chatbot include:

- Artificial Intelligence

- Natural Language Processing Capability

- Conversational Content Creator

- User Interface

As the team works to brainstorm all the resources they need, be sure to keep these questions top of mind and answer them very candidly:

- Consider if any technology is the product's "special sauce." A unique, proprietary type of technology would be an asset the company will want to own outright.

- If this technology is something that doesn't exist yet, does the company need to invent something new?

- Consider "the when", of your strategy: What can be accomplished and achieved here today versus near-term future and even longer-term future?

Once your team understands the scope, evaluate the list of identified resource needs against the current internal inventory of assets. Keep what you can afford, and the scope of your budget top of mind:

- What can be accomplished and achieved with the assets and abilities you have in-house?

- What can be bought? What can you afford?

- Does an existing company do this really well, and if so, could you either buy or partner with them?

- What skill sets will be required?

- What talent do you currently have in-house?

- Who do you have to recruit and hire?

With the lists fleshed out, keep track of the overlapping actions and duplicate or repeated resources. For example, scenes 1, 2, 3, and 5 all have a requirement for a chatbot. This should grab your attention. Actions that span multiple scenes require larger scrum teams and/or is a sign the technology could be worthy of becoming the product's special sauce. Continuing with a chatbot example, a key technical need for a fully operational chatbot is artificial intelligence (AI). AI is surely the product's special sauce and technology that company will want to own outright.

EMPHASIZE PRIORITIZATION

The last step is to organize the actions by effort level: light effort, medium effort, or heavy effort. And know that it's not expected that you have *all* the answers up front. That's the nature of this type of work.

There's a good chance you won't get a sizable team who has enough resources to tackle all the initiatives and respective actions identified at once (but kudos if you do). If you have limited resources at your disposal, emphasize prioritization. Perhaps prioritizing a light effort will help give your team a sense of accomplishment and build momentum. Prioritization will continually happen throughout the Visioneering process, but it's extremely important now, as your team is getting out of the gate.

BUILD THE TEAMS AND IDENTIFY INTERNAL RESOURCES

Now you understand the assets currently at your disposal; you've decided what you're going to do in-house versus outsourcing by identifying the personnel you have and who you need to hire. These are the decisions that inform your staffing plan. Now, you'll assign teams to perform the work.

PHASE 2: SET UP THE TEAMS

You know from experience that convincing senior stakeholders to fund a proper product vision was challenging. Now you face another challenge— to convince those same stakeholders to reexamine their product development team structure. Choose your words wisely! Most stakeholders will bristle at even the suggestion of a reorganization. Instead of using the word *re-org*, use the word *adapt*. The word adapt implies the current means are simply adjusting to new conditions:

Visioneering's adaptive structure will optimize an organization's internal resources and dovetail with the agile model development and scrum practices already in place.

What stakeholder wouldn't want that! Highlight within this new adaptive structure teams will have access to the right resources and expertise to solve the problem in front of them. And unlike the current structure—one that is a disconnected feature factory—teams will now clearly understand how to collaborate with one another. All of the barriers once standing in the way of problem solving, are now removed.

THE TRIAD

At the heart of the team structure is the product vision and the *triad*. The triad (**Figure 7.5**) includes the champions of the product vision and the leaders of the Visioneering process. The three members of a triad are the

B, E, and D of BEDRC: the product manager (B), the technology head (E) and the strategic designer (D). Every product vision must have a triad in place—no exceptions! The triad ensures that the teams are working independently toward delivering their respective actions while sharing what they've learned, coordinating, and collaborating on achieving the broader product vision.

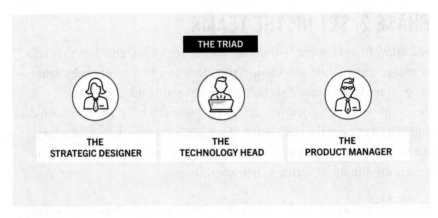

FIGURE 7.5 The triad.

Consider the descriptions of the three roles:

The product manager is effectively the CEO of the product vision endeavor and its related initiatives. They are data-driven and have a deep understanding of the needs of their target audience. When the team is at an impasse, unable to make a decision based on the evidence at hand, the product manager is the *decider*. When a vote ends up in a tie, they are the tiebreaker. They remove roadblocks, define measurable objectives, foster collaboration and transparency, and empower teams working on vision initiatives to make decisions about how best to deliver the work in their respective backlogs. Above all, the product manager is accountable for delivering outcomes that drive value to the business.

The technology head oversees and guides technology-related decisions made across all product vision initiatives. They work closely with technology leads from each scrum team to ensure engineering resources and development architecture are being used efficiently and effectively. The technology head has one foot in the present—making sure teams have the tools and resources to deliver near-term actions—and one foot in the future—focused on the technology required to achieve the experience outlined in the product vision.

The strategic designer's function (that's you!) in the triad keeps all initiatives and respective scrum teams focused on the experience tenets while keeping the target audience top of mind. They inspire teams to think big and take risks while navigating to the product vision. With first principles thinking, they're always looking for opportunities to identify, challenge, and validate assumptions. The strategic designer provides visionary guidance to all designers working on initiative teams, fosters collaboration and communication across teams, and guarantees that content and visual design are consistently on brand.

The triad must be supported by the core roles of content strategy and research (**Figure 7.6**).

FIGURE 7.6 The product vision and BEDRC core roles.

CONTENT STRATEGY

In most cases, the seasoned content strategist (the C in BEDRC), operates consultatively, supporting the triad and all delivery teams. Orchestrating the plan and directing the creation of impactful and consistent messaging across a variety of teams and initiatives. But depending on the capabilities and staffing structure of your business, you should assign individual writers to work on specific teams that have greater content creation needs (e.g., teams focused on marketing, communications, development of training material, or customer support). The content strategist would coordinate with every delivery team to support their content needs and ensure that the writing style and tone of voice remains consistent across all content being produced.

Consider this adaptive measure: for product vision work that relies very heavily on content production, the content strategist could be folded into the triad as honorary additional member.

RESEARCH

Similar to content strategy, research will play a critical role in guiding the journey to delivering your product vision. Ideally, the original researcher who participated as a core team member during your product strategy and vision development (the R of BEDRC) will remain in a consultative capacity to oversee a team of researchers dedicated to supporting the tactical delivery teams. The overall size of the research team dedicated to the work is relative to the size of the product vision and number of teams and initiatives they have to support. At a bare minimum, this is one person. The important thing here is consistency—having the same person or research team that understands the work being done is a huge advantage versus cycling in new researchers on a case-by-case basis.

Ultimately, research fuels the Visioneering process and becomes the thread that aligns tactical decisions across the multiple initiatives. Having a person or team who are consistently focused on the research needs of tactical teams working to the product vision makes your research efforts more efficient and effective. There is no need to continually onboard new research associates, getting them up to speed on the target audience and goals of the program. The work of the consultative research team is cumulative, building on itself to help guide the decisions and direction of the overall group. A dedicated team can also be more proactive about research needs, detecting opportunities to identify and debunk (or prove) assumptions.

THE EXPERIENCE PILLARS AND TEAMS

The key to producing work that is in the image of the product vision is to adapt the team's thinking and systematic approach to mirror the *structure* of a product vision. As you now know, the product vision is anchored in, and structured against, the four experience pillars (**Figure 7.7**).

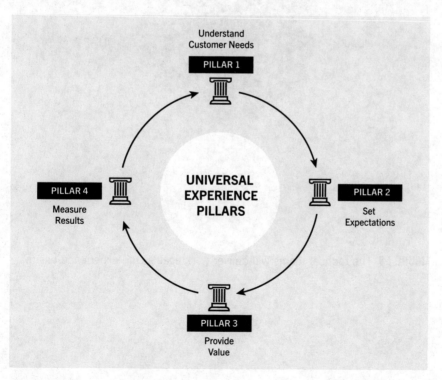

FIGURE 7.7 The four experience pillars.

See where we're going with this? Set up the tactical teams, each dedicated to one initiative. Each initiative will cyclically move through the four experience pillars (**Figure 7.8**). The experience pillars were covered in depth in Chapter 6, "Telling the Story of the Future Experience," so if you need a refresher, reread the relevant section in that chapter.

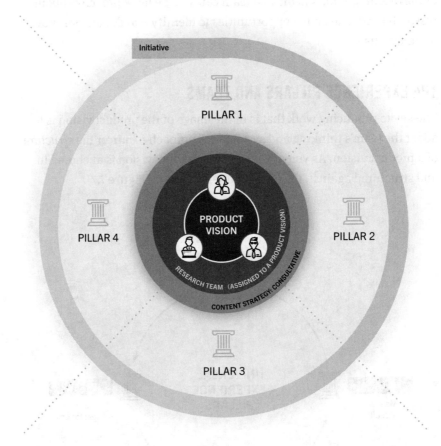

FIGURE 7.8 The tactical teams will deliver work against the experience pillars.

SCRUM TEAMS

Each initiative has at least one dedicated scrum team who works to deliver incrementally and continuously to develop, test, and launch product releases. Ideally this team is made up of between five and nine people. Each scrum team should be properly staffed and appropriately equipped to achieve their actions. Some actions will cross over between initiatives, and that's a good thing! These threads will require ongoing communication and cross-initiative teamwork and collaboration. The example illustrated here is a setup for an approximately 30-person-sized project, which is an average staffing for an important product at a medium-sized established business. Later in the section, we discuss scalability and how to size up considerably larger (a hundred plus persons), or considerably smaller, the extreme minimum (a setup of five persons).

Each team should be stable, meaning the teams stay together for as much time as possible and members are dedicated to one body of work. Stable teams are a good thing. Not only does a stable team build rapport, momentum, and develop predictability, but also the quality of the work will improve.

Every scrum team has a decider, the product owner (PO). The PO's skills may vary, but they always understand the strategy, the product vision, their role, goals and tactics, and how to track progress to goals. Each PO works closely with the triad to make sure their scrum team is aligned with the whole. If you're a strategic designer who understands how to measure success, then you too could be the product owner. Most scrum teams will also have a technology lead; the tech lead is the person most experienced in the technology that the scrum team is working on. For example, if your team is focused on native mobile application development, your tech lead is no less than a senior mobile developer. Some scrum teams will have a mini-triad in place: a PO, a design lead, and a tech lead. These mini-triads are a perfect environment for the tactical designer looking to get experience leveling up to be a strategic designer and eventually develop their own product vision. But every scrum team doesn't have to have a mini-triad. Staff appropriately to the goal. Here are the likely tactical roles your scrum teams may require:

- Tactical designers:

  - user interface design (UI)

  - interaction design (IxD)

- Full-stack developers

- Front-end developers

- Writers, copy editors

- Business analysts

- QA analysts

- Marketing specialists

For example, if the scrum team's action was backend and focused on a CRM, then the team is staffed with a PO, a tech lead, and a handful of full-stack developers. The scrum team is represented by the S in a circle (**Figure 7.9**), as shown in the full structure of the teams (**Figure 7.10**).

FIGURE 7.9 Key to future diagrams: the scrum team.

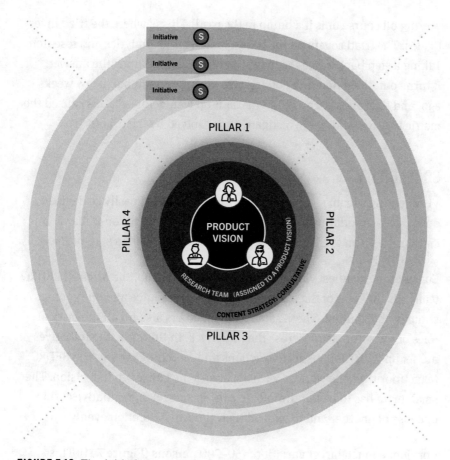

FIGURE 7.10 The initiatives and scrum team structure.

INVESTIGATIVE SERVICES

The triad is always available to scrum teams to investigate worrisome
metric results. For example: Let's say a scrum team defines a measurement
plan to capture daily sign-ups. The team actively tracks how many people
are signing up for the service, daily. Ten daily sign-ups are an indication
that you're on course—and as it turns out, the team achieves that bar, time
and time again. But then suddenly, that metric drops from ten daily sign-
ups to two daily sign-ups. What's going on? Does this indicate that you're

veering off course or is it a bump in the road? This is where the triad investigates. The triad covers all the bases, looking into analytics and research. Taking a step back to see the bigger picture, the triad finds the answer. It turns out, the marketing dollars were abruptly cut in half a few weeks ago, and the funds to campaign the sign-up were reduced. This caused the metric to drop. Another investigative case solved by the triad!

SCALABILITY

Visioneering's team structure allows for a business to easily scale up or down, accommodating any team size, from the multitrillion-dollar financial services firm to the newly established business with a staff of 25.

Consider the smallest variation. For the smallest team, the original BEDRC team fills the roles of the triad, one researcher resource and one content strategist consultant. These same team members also fill all the tactical roles of the scrum team across the initiatives. In this case, the initiatives are set up with their respective actions and marching orders. The BEDRC team prioritizes the work as a whole, across the entire product vision. The small team has to be mindful not to concentrate on one initiative at the expense of another and to expend their time and attention evenly.

Consider a much larger variation, 150–200 persons (**Figure 7.11**). This large team would have a triad, a well-staffed research team (4–8 people), consultative content strategists (4–8 people), and each initiative team has multiple scrum teams (each scrum team 5–9 people). On this larger team, the triad will have to modify their 1:1s—perhaps limiting them to as needed or scheduling them to be monthly rather than weekly. Alternatively, the triad could implement weekly, smaller, recurring group sessions with each of their respective disciplines. For example, the strategic designer has weekly recurring sessions with groups of tactical designers. A sizable team can also take advantage of *scrum-of-scrums*. Scrum-of-scrums are weekly, and participants are the collective product owners, or designated "ambassador," who meet to compare plans.

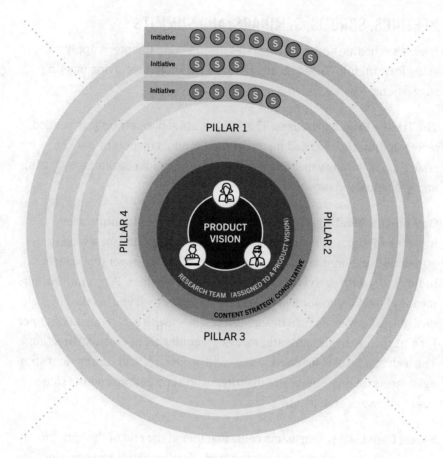

FIGURE 7.11 Scaling up the team.

AWARENESS

An initiative you may not think of, could be dedicated to *awareness*. This initiative, involves primarily marketing and keeps the marketing department looped in to all the product vision work. The awareness team is heavily staffed with marketing-oriented people, and this is especially true of the product owner. The PO knows that success looks like getting potential customers to the door and then into the funnel. The actions assigned to this team include advertising, email campaigns, commercials, and education.

MEETINGS: SCRUMS, SEMINARS, AND SUMMITS

A team's schedule and working styles discussed in Chapter 4 apply
going forward into Visioneering. Here are additional recurring meeting
suggestions.

The Triad + Product Owners. The triad meets separately only as needed.
More importantly, the triad meets with all product owners at weekly,
recurring, mandatory meetings to plan sprints, groom backlogs, check in,
and get status updates.

One-on-One Meetings. Outside of that larger sprint planning meeting, each of the triad members meet with their discipline for a weekly,
30-minute, one-on-one (1:1) meeting. The product manager (PM) meets
individually with each PO for a 1:1. Here, the PM helps a PO calibrate their
means of tracking to success. The same happens with you, as the strategic
designer, and your tactical designers. You meet with each tactical designer
for a 1:1 to provide design critique, design guidance, or creative direction.
The tech head meets for one-on-ones with each tech lead, the content strategist meets for one-on-ones with writers and copy editors and the same
goes for the research team.

Sprint Demo. All scrum teams come together at the end of the sprint to
demo what they've built or accomplished. Here's a handy presentation
format to follow; each team has a fixed amount of time—usually no more
than five minutes—to present the following (in this order):

1. Here's what we did.

2. Here's what we learned.

3. Here's how we measured success and measurements.

The research team should also have a time to present their findings.

PHASE 3: DELIVERY

For organizations new to the Visioneering approach, the idea of multiple empowered teams all defining and delivering their own products probably sounds like utter chaos. Fortunately, at this point you understand and possess the keys to success: a well-defined strategy and product vision combined with the triad working to foster communication, transparency, and alignment between teams. Just like the massive robot warrior Voltron comprises five powerful and individually operated gigantic lion robot spaceships, your teams work together yet independently until they ultimately come together to form a seamless and united product vision more powerful than the sum of its parts. So how exactly can individual teams of people successfully work independently together? In addition to great communication, transparency, and a clear direction provided by the product vision, techniques that will lead to Visioneering success include defining your outcomes and hypothesis.

CLEARLY DEFINE OUTCOMES

The teams' focus should be evident based on how they have been organized during the assessment phase. It's important when establishing the teams to do your best to make sure that their work isn't overlapping—or worse, redundant or even competing—with other teams in the group. The most effective way to do this is to make sure each team's outcomes are well defined.

Outcomes are the end results that each team is attempting to achieve. Outcomes naturally build step-by-step towards—*ladder up to*—the product goals and business objectives. For instance, a team focused on the initiative of gathering information about customers and their goals could be responsible for outcomes directly related to the methods, amount, and types of information gathered about their users. These outcomes may include a specific quantity of data that's being collected month after month, the team's ability to gather additional information over time, or enhancement of users' ability to easily share information.

Well-defined outcomes allow teams to experiment with a variety of solutions (with guidance and input from the triad) in order to achieve and improve on the outcomes for which they're responsible. Working within an outcomes-based model like this provides autonomy for teams to make their own decisions and control their own destiny. This approach leads to increased engagement from team members compared to teams who are simply taking orders and doing exactly what they've been told based on a product roadmap or laundry list of features to be delivered. As long as the outcomes are well defined, communication flows freely, and teams are grounded in the product vision, increased autonomy and engagement usually lead to more creative solutions to achieve the outcomes.

SPECIFY YOUR HYPOTHESES

In order for each team to develop the proposed solutions that will lead to achievement of the outcomes, it helps to start with clearly defined hypotheses. The hypotheses should be specified and shared with the triad and all delivery teams in your organization. Again, communication and transparency are paramount to successfully operate via the Visioneering process. This is especially true of large, complex businesses with many layers and divisions—*matrixed* businesses. In these sprawling enterprises you'll too often find teams working in silos on very similar initiatives. You want to avoid this by ensuring that your teams' hypotheses are stated clearly and well understood among all teams working toward your product vision (sharing with product teams in your business that aren't focused on the product vision work can also be useful).

The following syntax is an effective way to define a hypothesis:

> We believe *[the specific action the team will take]*

> For *[a specific user in a specific context]*

> Will result in *[an outcome or step leading to an outcome that the team has been assigned]*

Here's an example of a hypothesis statement with the blanks filled in where the team is responsible for the outcome of increasing user registration:

We believe creating a fun, four-question survey for customers who are considering signing up for our service will result in users being able to understand how our service can help them achieve their goals, leading to increased user sign-ups.

Ideally, any team's hypothesis is clear enough for everyone involved to understand the proposed solution they're going to be working on, the intended audience, and the expected outcome. Again, sharing the hypothesis and gathering feedback from the triad and the other tactical delivery teams is imperative. Another team may have already tried a similar approach. What can you learn from what they did? Another team may be building a complementary data-collection engine that will give you a head start. How can you join forces? The triad will also likely have opinions about how the solution could be executed in accordance with the broader product vision. They can also help to make sure teams have the resources they need to deliver on the hypothesis.

DEFINE YOUR MVP (MEANS OF VALIDATING A HYPOTHESIS)

With outcomes and hypotheses clearly understood and agreed on, the next step is for the individual teams to define their MVP. When talking about product development, the initials MVP stand for *minimum viable product*. This was originally intended to mean delivering the fewest features to a customer base in order to gather feedback that will influence future iterations of the product. The term was originally coined in 2001 by Frank Robinson and became more commonly known through the writing of Eric Ries, primarily via his blog and the publication of his book, *The Lean Startup in 2011* (Currency, 2011). Since then, businesses small and large all over the world have adopted and horribly misused the term.

Sadly, many businesses have interpreted MVP simply to mean the first version of a product that they're launching. This may be due, in part, to people's subjective understanding of the words *minimum* and *viable*. When it comes to clarifying the number of features a product should include, one person's definition of minimum can easily differ from another's. In terms of viability, what actually makes something viable? And is it viable to the business or to the end user? This confusion often leads businesses to launch "MVPs" with feature bloat, a lack of clear understanding about what users want or need, and no explicit way of collecting customer feedback.

For our purposes, with apologies to Eric Ries, here are alternate words for the letters MVP that will help guide the Visioneering process. Instead of a minimum viable product, think of your MVP as an experiment—the *Means* of *Validating* a hy*Pothesis*. At this point, with your team's well-defined objectives and hypothesis, it's time to define the MVP experiment that the team will create to validate that hypothesis. This is an opportunity for the team to be creative. Depending on the hypothesis, the MVP could take many forms; it doesn't necessarily have to be a fully developed and functional feature or product. Determine the most effective and efficient (think minimal again) way to prove your hypothesis. Perhaps you could use a nonfunctional prototype, build a marketing landing page, or even launch a survey to quickly get the feedback needed by the team. For example, scene 1 of the product vision illustrates the use of a chatbot. But of course, a fully operational, artificially intelligent chatbot may not be achievable out of the gate. So, consider the intention your team is hoping to ultimately fulfill: a conversation between the company and the user. The first version of this could take the form of a phone call to a customer representative. Your team will decide the best initial implementation to meet the objective.

Be sure to share your MVP approach with the triad and the other teams, and get busy building your solution.

The product goals and business objectives likely won't change much as teams work through the Visioneering process toward the longer-term product vision—but the hypothesis and MVPs certainly should. Sprint after sprint, teams will create new or tweak existing hypotheses, define and run experiments (MVPs), and collect results. Those MVPs will be demoed and the results will be shared across the teams to inform future work— that is, the next round of hypotheses and MVPs. This process repeats and cumulatively builds upon itself. Each team works independently, yet collaboratively and transparently, toward meeting their specific outcomes.

LET GO OF PERFECTION

When you've embraced an iterative, objectives-oriented delivery process, it's important to abandon the ideals of perfection in favor of deciding when something is "good enough." Too often, in a more traditional delivery model, designers know that once a product or feature has launched, their odds of being able to go back and make changes or improvements are low. Typically, when the product goes out the door, making any incremental enhancements is impossible because the team has moved on to a new challenge. This inability to make future fixes causes us to dig in our heels about interactions and design details that other team members (product owners and developers) may see little value in. It drives us to do our best to make sure a design is as perfect as possible before it's considered done.

While quality is still imperative, Visioneering allows teams to relax some of the standards because they can be confident that if a design detail didn't make it into the current iteration, there will always be another opportunity coming up. It helps to get into the habit of asking teammates whether something is good enough. This can be done in any team activity—especially if you're beginning to notice that the team is swirling or having trouble moving forward decisively. Push the team toward good enough and remind them that there's always another opportunity to make improvements.

OPERATING THE COMPASS

It's time to prove the value of the navigating by compass over a roadmap. Here's how it works. You now have multiple tactical teams assigned to each of the initiatives that are cranking out assigned, prioritized actions. In a nutshell, in each sprint, a tactical scrum team hypothesizes, tests, refines, and launches a small contribution—and puts a respective measurement plan in place to objectively determine whether or not their small contribution was successful:

- Did it work?

- Did it provide value to the customer?

- Did it meet agreed-on goals and objectives?

A successful contribution strengthens the value-based partnership between the company and the customer. But aside from proving their success (or not), the team learns something in the process and applies that knowledge going forward. Here's where the triad comes in. The triad keeps a distant eye on the happenings, learnings and results of each sprint. This is easily done from afar, because all the teams are open about what they're measuring and how they're tracking to success. But the triad can't get stuck in the weeds. They have to keep perspective. The triad's job is to utilize the compass—navigating by metrics, because metrics ladder up to initiatives, objectives and big goals. So, whereas each scrum team is focused on single-metric results for an individual contribution, the triad is focused on monitoring, analyzing, and interpreting the accumulated metric results across all initiatives and the collective contributions. The accumulated metric results indicate to the triad whether the body of work is achieving the product vision and, ultimately, chipping away at high-level goals. Alternatively, the results could indicate that the body of work has veered off course and is need of course correction, or that the entire effort needs to pivot.

To visualize this, imagine a physical compass. The compass's cardinal directions are clearly marked: the top of the compass is north; to the right, east, and to the left, west. At the bottom of the compass is south. In-between each direction are degrees, or tick marks. Your triad sets the compass needle to due north, aligning their product vision to their North Star, their product bound to a purposeful direction. Out of the gate, during the first sprint, the scrum teams produce metric results that, thankfully, prove successful. The needle, set due north, doesn't flinch. The work is on course. Ideally, a good run will produce consecutive sprints that yield successful results—that needle doesn't flinch. But eventually, a scrum team produces unsuccessful results. The needle pings one degree to the right. Uh-oh, what's happening? Is this a blip on the radar that will resolve itself? A single metric has limited insight. So, the triad won't be able to see the impact of the metric results every sprint. As a few sprints go by, the metric results across multiple teams begin to indicate that our actions are proving unsuccessful—i.e. the scrum teams' efforts are not helping to achieve our outcomes. The needle banks hard to the right, pointing northeast. The triad needs to figure out if the metrics are just indicating the work is veering off course or if they are the first signs that the entire effort is failing and needs to pivot. Most likely, the work is veering off course. If the product vision is done well, the need to pivot won't happen often.

So, at quarterly intervals the triad pauses to:

1. Evaluate

2. Make an informed decision

3. Coordinate next steps

With every evaluation, the triad can then make an informed decision (to stay the course, course-correct, or pivot) and coordinate next steps.

EVALUATE

By regularly evaluating the accumulated metrics, the triad will know whether or not the work is delivering on the product vision, whether the product vision still matters, and it continues to be in alignment with its North Star. Every quarter, the triad will be able to see the larger effect of the cumulative results. It is then that they pause to ask the big question, "Are we still moving in a purposeful direction?" Here are the questions you will want to answer.

On executing the intention of the product vision (or not):

- Are we delivering on the story of the experience?

- Is this still the right experience for our customer?

- Has the product landscape changed?

- Does the product still give the company a competitive edge?

But what if a few people on the team are convinced that their approach is laddering up to the product vision, but others disagree? The metrics should speak to whether or not the work is on course. But sometimes there is a level of interpretation that can cause a gray area. Ultimately, if there needs to be a decider, the product manager has the final word.

Check your North Star. As the work builds, it will be all too easy to lose sight of *why* you're doing what you're doing.

On whether or not the product continues to be in alignment with its North Star:

- Does this product further the company's mission?

- Does this product achieve the expressed goals and business objectives?

- Does this product serve the company's vision? Help the business get one step closer to the company they want to become?

- Is the product reflective of the brand's core values and principles?

Lastly, it's important to check whether the team's thinking strives to be innovative. We pushed you to produce an innovative product vision. But hey, a truly innovative vision is far and few in between. An innovative product or service is novel, different; it changed the game. If you're not Jeff Bezos, you may have fallen short—and that's okay. If your product work creates a value-based partnership and is, overall, a good offering, then that's a success. Just keep striving to think innovatively. You'll know whether the team is doing this, because everyone will be *uncomfortable*.

On whether or not the team is striving to be innovative:

- Are we comfortable, complacent? Are things easy?

- Are we pushing ourselves?

MAKE A DECISION

As the wave of results come into focus, one of three decisions will have to be made:

- Stay the course, with the same actions, needs, and priorities.

- Course-correct, reassess actions and needs, then adjust priorities.

- Pivot.

If the hypotheses are proving successful, faring the way the teams predicted, then stay the course and keep the priorities as is. But maybe the way you thought this would go is just not working. In that case, the learnings do support the product vision, but not the interpretation of how the product vision comes together. Here, you would reassess the various actions, and respective resources. Or you may decide you need to pivot. It's not a complete failure, such is the nature of this work. Perhaps the team set out building x, but as it turns out, testing is proving customers don't necessarily want x. Perhaps the opportunity space was upended by a brand-new competitor and the bar of what's considered innovative is reset. When this happens, delivery is selectively paused while the core team returns to the product vision process. With the strategy, all five strategic building blocks are regroomed, and then the experience story is tweaked, the prototype altered, the work validated, and the deliverable updated. Only then, with a fresh product vision, is the delivery fully resumed.

COORDINATE NEXT STEPS

If the decision is to stay the course, with no change to tactical needs, then there will be no interruption to delivery. If that's not the case, there is time that is taken away from teams delivering output. The decision to reassess the initiatives, actions, and resources may ask for a brief hiatus that requires three to five business days of work—depending on the breadth of the assessment. A decision to pivot will cause a significant interruption to delivery. Stakeholders will need to sign off on pivots, so regular meetings to lay the groundwork before a seismic shift happens will help. These pauses are a good opportunity to share and update your senior stakeholders with all that's happening. And make sure they are in agreement. Know that stakeholders are interested in the what and the why, not the *how*. So, whatever you do, don't get into the tactical details. Pro tip: Every senior stakeholder has their own agenda. Find out what those goals and agenda look like and weave them into your talking points.

WHEN LOST...

What happens when a team stops using their compass and loses their way? Most likely, the first sign will be your team will have returned to operate as a feature factory. They're simply going through the motions. No one knows why the features matter anymore; they're just cranking out a list of features! Everyone has lost the connections to outcomes and providing customer value. This will be the first sign. The second sign may be that the teams aren't able to clearly see how to measure success. They will have lost the clear understanding of why the work that they're doing matters or what goals they're serving. These are both good indicators that you're lost and ultimately, why Visioneering matters: being accountable to deliver work that your team, business, and customers actually care about. On that note, the next chapter covers how to sell your organization on the value of cementing the Visioneering process as the defacto way of doing things.

CHAPTER 8
BUILDING YOUR VISIONEERING PRACTICE

By now your team is well underway successfully executing your product vision, masterfully navigating uncharted terrain with a trusty compass and maintaining a clear view of your North Star. The results are proof that the Visioneering process works! But old ways and bad habits die hard. Individuals on your scrum teams may be tempted to fall back to the comforting familiarity of product roadmaps, legacy thinking, and "feature factory" mindsets. Enforce a regimented Visioneering practice—be strict, until it sticks. The goal will be to cement the Visioneering practice as the accepted way of working on your team, within the broader product program and ultimately across the wider organization. Visioneering has a much higher acceptance rate if a company embraces and supports it. This will take a commitment on your part to evangelize Visioneering by routinely making your way up to the pulpit to preach and spread the gospel.

You can tastefully do this by writing an objective, fact-based case study and then using that case study as your primary marketing tool. Alongside the case study, two other major selling points are:

- Visioneering elevates a company's design maturity (a key competitive advantage).

- Visioneering positively influences company culture.

And as you're doing all of this evangelizing to improve and better the company you're employed at, don't forget to look out for number one! That's you and your needs. You can apply Visioneering to improve and better your personal and career development as a designer. This chapter will help you achieve all of this. Here's how to set yourself up.

EVANGELIZING VISIONEERING

To effectively spread the gospel, first write a case study. It's now about selling both this new way of doing things and yourself, the strategic designer. The strategic designer is crucial to the creation of the strategy-led product vision, the heart of the Visioneering process and key to success. So, if you want to sell Visioneering, you have to talk about you. In turn, talking about the good work that you're doing will help to grow your career. You, the product vision and Visioneering are now forever intertwined. A case study is an extremely effective way of selling all three of these things.

What is a case study? Quite simply, a case study is a means of sharing the results of your work and the process by which you went about doing it—the "from, to." Case studies are often used by designers to build their portfolios, and they're provided to potential clients as a part of most agencies' pitch and proposal presentations. Case studies go beyond merely sharing stunning but superficial visuals to tell a compelling story of how and why the work was done. Creating a case study is another opportunity to practice your storytelling skills and a perfect way to evangelize the Visioneering process within your organization.

A CASE STUDY FORMAT

Just like the structure used to create your experience story, an effective case study has a fairly standard format: define the problem, show the process, present the results and issue a call to action (**Figure 8.1**).

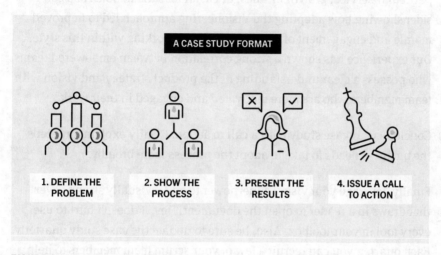

A CASE STUDY FORMAT

1. DEFINE THE PROBLEM

2. SHOW THE PROCESS

3. PRESENT THE RESULTS

4. ISSUE A CALL TO ACTION

FIGURE 8.1 A case study format.

Start by defining the problem that you've solved. In our case, the problem is most likely related to the challenges of working within the feature factory mentality, such as delivering uninspired products, executing a list of features without a clear purpose, a lack of innovation, heavy priority on the business's over the users' needs, and an unengaged workforce.

Next, show the process. Share key examples of how you received backing from executive leadership, formed the BEDRC team, defined the product strategy, produced the product vision, and used the Visioneering process to incrementally deliver value to the business and your target audience. Include what you learned along the way about how long each step took, how much each team member was involved, challenges the team experienced, and examples of specific techniques that worked to make the process successful. Share any obstacles that your team encountered along the way and how you overcame them.

Step 3 is to present the results as they relate to the original problem (or problems) that you described at the beginning. This presentation should most certainly include metrics related to the success of the product. These may include an increase in the number of customers signing up for a particular service, growth in sales, or customer satisfaction. Also consider showing how adopting the Visioneering approach led to improved morale and engagement of the team members working within this style. Our experience has shown a strong correlation between empowered teams who possess a clear understanding of the product strategy and vision with team members who are more motivated and engaged in their work.

Conclude your case study with a call to action. Clearly explain any steps the business needs to take to adopt the process more broadly.

Finally, leverage your visual superpower to add a visually strong cover that draws in a reader to open the document. Hey, it doesn't hurt to use every tool in your toolbox. Also, be sure to update the case study quarterly. Each quarter, you can recruit a few of your scrum team members to help you do that. This exercise will be a constant reminder to your team why you do things this way.

ADDRESSING PRODUCT VISION DEFICIT

Where can Visioneering help next? The most immediate next step likely involves identifying other product and service candidates within the organization that can use this type of help. Tread lightly! You are being asked to critique your colleagues' work. Yes, it's true that those not practicing strategic product vision and Visioneering are probably in desperate need of strategic thinking and a better approach—but of course, your colleagues might think otherwise. They probably think they are doing a stellar job! The trick will be to allow others to naturally come to the conclusion that product vision and Visioneering is the better path forward. The case study will greatly help with this.

With the case study in hand—your Visioneering brochure—the triad sets out to *sell* other teams and colleagues on this better way of working. Schedule casual meetings with team leads who are interested in learning more about your success. If you can, recruit your triad peers to come with you. If all goes as planned, your colleagues will ask you how their teams, with products live in market, can leverage Visioneering. You can respond with "What a great question, I'm so glad you asked!" A product or service without a strategy-led product vision has what's called product vision deficit. These teams with products already in market, cannot just move forward, as is, into Visioneering. They will have to first retrofit their product or service with a strategy-led product vision before they move into Visioneering. But you can certainly advise them on that!

Some teams will have an easier time doing this than others. A product or service with severe product vision deficit will not be difficult to spot for the trained eye of the strategic designer. The most desperate of cases have all of the hallmark signs—the offering lacks clear business objectives, vaguely addresses user problems, and misaligns with their company's mission. These are the product teams lost working in "feature factories," tirelessly spinning their wheels, working in circles, and often carelessly heading off in any direction. These teams have a lot of work to do. Perhaps starting at the very beginning, learning the difference between tactical designer versus a strategic designer, and the importance of strategy. In less severe cases, an experienced team will have done a really good job on the strategy portion, likely having identified most of the strategic building blocks. But then fell by not translating the strategy into a proper vision. In this instance, deficit can be addressed in a shorter time period. Either way, deficit is corrected by a team first pausing delivery. Then address any limiting beliefs or stale thinking—that has to go. With a renewed perspective and sense of excitement for the work, deficit is similar to a pivot. Return to phase 1 of the product vision process. Help your colleagues set up a core BEDRC team, establish their team contract, working agreement, and values. A laboratory environment will need to be created, and the team will have to find their rhythm. Finding their rhythm may take some patience as they adjust to this different mindset. Remind your colleagues to use this time as an opportunity to reset. That means making sure to validate all the information and assumptions they are working with. Validate, validate, validate. Then you are hands off, acting simply as a cheerleader from the sidelines, cheering them on as they sequentially move through the remaining three phases of the product vision process. Only when the product vision process is thoroughly completed, can they move into Visioneering.

ACTING AS AN INTERNAL CONSULTANT

If you choose, the strategic designer can act as trusted product vision and Visioneering *internal consultant* (**Figure 8.2**). But be forewarned that if you choose to set up this hotline, it will be ringing off the hook, because after a business witnesses Visioneering success, they will want to replicate that success and they will want to do it fast. Your instinct will be to get involved and help everyone. But acting as an internal consultant is extra work that will be piled on top of your existing Visioneering triad responsibilities. Know that it will be challenging to find time to do both and do them well.

FIGURE 8.2 Opportunities for an internal consultant.

If you do choose to act as a consultant, here are some tasks where you can lend your expertise, on a case-by-case basis:

Assist in vetting vision proposals, and for those that are worthy of a product vision endeavor, help set up a new project. If the team is new to product visions, they will need help securing the right resources to be set up for success. Per Visioneering, you can offer to coach new triads, assist in assessing staffing needs and hiring. At any time, you can offer to aid stakeholders by accompanying them to review sessions, sprint demos or proposal presentations to weigh in on critical decisions.

Now that you are a trusted adviser, you will advise stakeholders on what to do and also what *not* to do. For example, convince stakeholders not to destabilize teams. The impulse of the business will be to replant the three triad members onto other projects. But removing the three individuals who are manning the compass will have devastating effects on a Visioneering endeavor. Instead of relocating to another team, offer other teams the opportunity to *shadow* yours. Shadowing is one of the most effective ways a strategic designer can help teach. After all, the best way to learn Visioneering is to watch a successful team practice it in action. Invite outsiders to come see your demos and immerse themselves in this new way of doing things. But be clear that onlookers can't distract your team from the work or disrupt meetings. Save questions until the end of the day or for another designated time. You can also set up online meetups to help facilitate training. Meetups are like professional clubs but without the uncool stigma. Participants of meetups share an interest, connected by a topic or activity. Set up a meetup on the topic of Visioneering. This is a great channel for sharing knowledge and onboarding those who are new to the process. Encourage scrum team members, and especially your tactical designer staff, to participate.

HELP ME, HELP YOU

Business and executive stakeholders who have adopted this new way of working will want to know what else they can do to *help* build the product vision and Visioneering practice. How's that for change! You should suggest creating a dedicated team that assesses the company's big picture. Beyond any one product is the company's collective offerings. Suggest developing a comprehensive inventory of all offerings, products, and services and how all the pieces either connect or don't connect—because the work doesn't stop and start at the singular product vision. The business's higher responsibility is to keep tabs on all products, their place, and their contribution to the bigger picture. Your scrum teams shouldn't be guessing where overlap exists and how each vision fits into a whole. The executive level should be able to speak to this. An informed picture will help Visioneering efforts coordinate across multiple product visions and possibly see where visions will intertwine in the near future. It may even be helpful to see not only the current product landscape, but reference past products and understand their demise so that history doesn't repeat itself. Over time, and many projects, you as the strategic designer and your fellow triad peers will gain knowledge that can help executives understand how different visions overlap. The executives will want your wisdom and guidance to connect the bigger picture dots. Yes, give your two cents and advice, but make sure to hold them responsible for this work.

PROMOTE FROM WITHIN

What better way to evangelize Visioneering than to promote those who are already drinking the vision Kool-Aid? You, a member of the triad, can promote from within your scrum teams. By investing in the team you hired and growing team members, you've ensured that they will, in return, preach the gospel, develop a sense of ownership, be more engaged, and commit to seeing the work through the challenging times. Which will be invaluable . . . because the work will get challenging! Assist tactical designers to level up to become design leads, and if they desire, embark on their own pilgrimage to become a strategic designer. As a former tactical designer yourself, you know they will be looking for coaches and mentors. Now, you can be one. It's true that not all of us are cut out to be mentors, but arguably, everyone can be a coach. You know which skills a promising tactical designer should be developing, so offer them the opportunity to watch you in action. Even an hour of your time will help a tactical designer, who often get caught in the weeds in ground-level contributing skills, to pick their head up and see the bigger picture.

Encourage your triad peers to do the same: the product manager should be grooming product owners for career development and the technology head should be promoting tech leads.

CONTRIBUTING TO A COMPANY'S DESIGN MATURITY

Visioneering is a key competitive advantage and can be a pathway to companies developing their design maturity. Within a Visioneering team, the act of designing and delivering a great user experience transcends any individual role. User experience isn't up to any single person or department. Creating valuable user experiences becomes a practice shared by each and every member of the team, and the importance of meeting users' needs is on par with meeting business objectives. Embracing a user-centric mentality throughout an organization is the embodiment of design maturity.

The adoption of this user-centric mentality matters to designers and their employers for two primary reasons:

- It elevates designers and the design process, putting you on equal footing with your technology and business peers.

- A user-centric mentality is good for business.

It matters to you and your peers as designers because working in this way has allowed you to ascend beyond simply being perceived by your business and technology colleagues as decorators. The majority of businesses are immature when it comes to how they view design. They generally employ designers to improve the aesthetics (and possibly the usability) of their existing products. This is design as decoration—the stage where many professional designers begin their career. Your journey from tactical to strategic designer doesn't just have the potential to elevate you personally, giving you a seat at the strategy table. It has the ability to elevate an organization's entire design practice by opening up the design process, making it accessible and visible to all.

This may sound like a bad idea to many designers, and some may resist it. Some may ask, "Why would we want to lift the veil on the creative process? Why would we want to include business and technology partners, allowing them access and influence over how the sausage gets made? Doesn't inviting nondesigners into the process cheapen the value of design as a whole?" In our experience, the answer to all these questions is an emphatic no. Keeping designers separate, treating them like oddball "creatives" who can't possibly understand the complexities of business and technology, is a disservice to all parties—just like excluding nondesigners from sharing in our approach to user-centered design prevents business and technology partners from understanding the financial value of building empathy and focusing on satisfying customers' needs. Cultivating a user-centric mentality throughout an organization has benefits to all parties involved, especially the designers who move beyond being perceived simply as decorators to become stewards of the Visioneering process and user-centric design.

Reason number two that adopting a user-centric mentality matters is that it has been shown to benefit business's bottom line. In fact, an October 2018 report by renowned international consulting firm McKinsey & Company indicated that the revenues and shareholder returns increased significantly for businesses that embrace user-centricity, measure design performance, embrace iterative delivery, and break down silos between physical, digital, and service design. The companies that are embodying these Visioneering themes the most effectively are seeing far greater business results than their peers.[1]

If delivering better products and increasing profits weren't enough of a reason to build your company's Visioneering capabilities, there are additional benefits that can positively influence a corporate culture and improve overall employee engagement.

CULTURE MATCH

Adopting this transparent, collaborative, and results-driven framework can help to transform an organization's mindset to influence the culture— and in return a culture's support will help a Visioneering practice thrive. So, what exactly is company culture? A culture is a company's core values and behavior attributes that shape the working environment. A good culture fit is important to retaining good people, creating working synergy, and reducing turnover. For our purposes, the ideal company culture is one that embraces the same values that Visioneering is rooted in:

- Encourages high levels of autonomy

- Champions boldness

- Fosters mindful collaboration

- Embraces calculated flexibility (friendly to exploration and experimentation)

- Is outcome oriented

---

1 www.mckinsey.com/business-functions/mckinsey-design/our-insights/
the-business-value-of-design

ASSESS THE COMPANY'S CULTURE

A company's culture will influence how smoothly Visioneering works. The closer your company's current culture aligns with those ideal values listed earlier, the smoother the ride. But the further away your company's current culture is from those ideal values, the bumpier the ride, and the odds of your Visioneering endeavor succeeding exponentially lessens. To the extreme, a company whose culture opposes these values completely can even be the cause of project failure. This oppositional culture can be recognized by their telltale signs: operates by command and control, is steeped in fear of failure, is task-oriented, and promotes *Hunger Games*–like internal competition (employee pitted against employee). A less than favorable culture can also be seen in colleagues' everyday attitude and the expression on their faces. If they exhibit low morale, lack empathy, and are gossipy, odds are that company doesn't uphold our idea Visioneering values! Hey, we have high standards. So, it's important you determine what kind of culture you are operating in. Perform an informal assessment of the company culture you're working in—if only for your own use.

First, obtain a copy of the company's expressly defined cultural style, likely posted to the company's website. A company has to define the desired culture to nurture and protect it. Having said that, be wary of a company that does not have articulated core values or cultural style. If leadership hasn't taken the time to articulate the culture they desire, chances are they just don't care. With a culture statement in hand, compare what's described on paper to reality. Is it the same? It may not be! Overall you have to evaluate the gap between what's defined and what's taking place and determine whether the gap is surmountable. If the culture is really toxic, then influencing a culture to effect change will be impossible. The good news is the problem isn't you, it's them. In this case, consider taking your talent elsewhere—life's short and you've got options. On the other hand, if you determine the culture to be less than favorable but there are reasons to stay and the company has promise (e.g., good people, platform-and-career-making opportunities are present), then influencing culture change with Visioneering is possible.

CORE COMPONENTS

No company is beyond redemption, and every company can turn their culture around for the better. But know that a single person can't change an entire culture by themselves. Complete culture transformation is a monumental task and doesn't happen overnight. Generally, it is established and enforced from the very top at the most senior executive level downward. However, you can highlight how the Visioneering model can help facilitate a more ideal culture by championing two core cultural components: driving higher engagement and encouraging a learning-friendly environment. These two components are drivers that create grassroots movements of culture change. The synergy from grassroots movements captures the attention of leadership, who can drive big culture change.

Engagement

Visioneering is a lever that you can pull to facilitate more *engagement* (**Figure 8.3**). What is engagement? A misconception about engagement is that it speaks to participation, that you showed up, whether you wanted to or not. A highly engaged employee is committed, invested, and motivated.

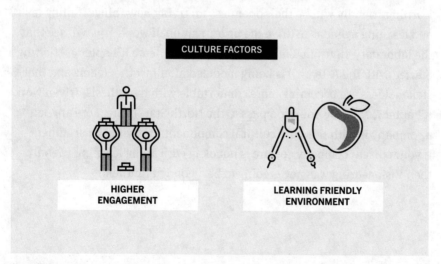

FIGURE 8.3 Engagement and friendliness to learning are key factors.

They're not just a bystander, putting in the lowest amount of effort to get by. If you are engaged, you like your job, you care about the work that's being done, and you're invested in seeing the work through to the end. A big part of Visioneering is the empowerment and autonomy it provides to the teams—this is where high engagement stems from. Your scrum team staff know they have the power to make decisions that matter; they are clear on their roles, know what success should look like, and are clear on the direction the team is heading in because the strategy and vision have been shared with them. This all results in high engagement—the corporate Holy Grail.

A good way of measuring engagement is to send out a questionnaire to your design staff on a quarterly basis. A number of firms, such as Gallup, offer these type of polling services to companies.

Learning friendly

If your company's leadership is open to embracing the Visioneering style of experimentation, exploration, and learning, then this is a great indicator of bigger change to come. Signs that a company is becoming more learning-friendly will be their openness to: trying new things, failing fast, and learning agendas to drive the prioritization of work. You will see that the laboratory environment you created for your team (Chapter 4, "Getting Started with the A-Team") is being modeled after by other teams and that stakeholders are becoming more comfortable with hypothesis-driven work (Chapter 7, "Setting Your Compass to the North Star"). The more aligned a company is with this core cultural component, the better. Disclaimer: If your current company culture is not okay with being learning-friendly, then Visioneering was never going to be a good fit for them!

DESIGNING INSIDE THE BOX

How do you design a culture that embraces collaboration and autonomy?

The objective is to create an environment where great talent can do great work, together. Culture comes not from focusing on the output but from hyper-focusing on the environment. The same level of curation needs to exist in selecting a diverse and cohesive team as there is in selecting the problems that the team will solve.

A strong culture is often the result of strong communication. Without frequent and open communication, "collaboration" and "autonomy" begin to contradict one another. In healthy cultures, it becomes self-evident that autonomy is as much a group activity as collaboration. The opportunity lies within developing a strong balance between push and pull. A high-impact team thrives when it mutually pushes against the status quo to pull in more (collective) creativity, while at the same time pushing against one another to pull the best out of each other.

One of the hardest aspects to reconcile about autonomy is the inherent nature of its necessity for accountability and for that accountability to be in and of itself collaborative. For a team to work well together, it must win together—which means it must be structured to lose together. It's important to remember that autonomy isn't given; it's taken away. We're autonomous by nature; we are each our own person with our own thoughts, fears, experiences, and ambitions. Collaboration brings that collective experience together to make something bigger and better than the sum of its parts. Autonomy simply removes as many of the constraints as possible to allow the collaborative to collaborate. Bring the right people together to solve the right problem at the time right time and then get out of the way.

— MARTIN RINGLEIN, CEO & CO-FOUNDER, PROMOTED

THE DESIGNER: ALWAYS EVOLVING

Ask yourself, are you comfortable? That feeling of unease is the strategic designer's sweet spot, a signal that we're doing our best work. So, if the answer is yes, you've become comfy cozy, then it's time to get uncomfortable again. Begin searching for new ways to level yourself up. You should be continuously striving to become better! Consider the late Neil Peart, the drummer from Rush. This epic musician remained at the top of his game by continually working to improve his craft, resetting the bar to reach higher and higher. He did this by seeking out advice and guidance from other experts in his field that could lend a new set of skills and different perspective. Like Peart, there's no limit to how great a designer you can be!

Thankfully you've figured out that the discipline of design is your profession of choice. The question now becomes, what's your vision for *yourself*? This may sound deep, but you can use the product vision and Visioneering process to guide your own personal development, push your skills to the next level, and execute your career plan. Here's how to do just that.

1. Make a Moodboard

First, just like with a vision proposal, create an inspirational moodboard. A career coach could also refer to this as your dream board. There are many online mood board offerings available, for free. Begin by asking yourself "what if . . . " and allow yourself to dream big. Use images and descriptive text. Don't filter the images, elements, or words that you are compelled to include. After the moodboard is complete, look for obvious patterns and different themes that emerge. Think about what the insights truly mean to you and how you feel about them. Feelings are important—they allow your subconscious to have a say!

2. Create a strategy

No matter where you are in your professional time line, it's never too late to create a career strategy. Answer the five strategic building blocks: the where, who, what, why, and when.

Consider the industry, sector, or area (the where) that excites and inspires you. Where do you want to invest your precious time, talent, and attention? You are the focus (the who). Your career (the what) lives at the intersection of the where and the who. Predict the timing (the when) that you estimate it will take you to acquire the necessary skills, education, and experience to achieve this optimal career experience. Finally, clarify how your ideal career aligns with your personal mission and purpose (the why). Even go so far as mapping out measurable objectives and signals that may indicate you're on the path toward success.

As you work through each building block, the test of whether a block is complete is the strength of its adherence to the whole. And again, try not to get hung up on how you will achieve these aspirations—that comes later.

3. Create an experience story

This is always the fun part. Translate your strategy by telling the story of a future experience. Create your own storyboard wall at home and frame out your story, scene by scene.

4. Acceptance

After you've gone through all the steps and created your vision for yourself, let it go—if just for a few weeks. After some time has passed, ask yourself, *is this really what you want?* Does the idea still excite you? Too many times we do what we think we should or do what others want. It is all too often that we find ourselves a few decades into a career and we haven't yet accomplished personally meaningful goals. Another confusing aspect is being clear on what you want for yourself versus what you believe others want for you. That line fast becomes blurry. Here's how you can get some clarity: show your vision to close friends, trusted colleagues, and family members. Does the vision you created resonate with who they know you to be? Does it align with what they believe are your personal values? These are the people who know you well and will be a good sounding board. A great response is "This is what you've always talked about!" or "This reminds me of the dreams that excited you as a kid!"

5. Visioneering you

Now leverage the Visioneering process to execute your professional dreams. Importantly, clearly define your North Star. What's your purpose?

Begin the Visioneering process. Start with an assessment. It may be helpful to ask a trusted colleague to help you do this, acting as a fresh pair of eyes and adding perspective. Break the vision down into actions and resources. Once you understand your needs, you can staff against it—or in this case, find the resources, teachers and recruit coaches to help you. For example, perhaps a higher level of expertise requires additional schooling specific certifications, or training. Perhaps you will need to network with specialized experts, which could be done at local conferences and messaging contacts via social networks like LinkedIn. Going forward, with priorities set, you carve out a thin slice of the vision and act on it. As you work through each iterative pass, keep the experience pillars top of mind. First, always understand your needs. Any way you slice it, it's imperative to keep your finger on the pulse of your ever-evolving needs. Then, set achievable and clear expectations. You will increase your confidence and have a better outcome when expectations are clearly set. When expectations have been set, it's time to deliver and ultimately, measure your results. Which brings us full circle back to understand your needs. Like with a product vision, as you continually measure and analyze your results, you will better understand yourself, your aspirations and modify how to move forward.

GET SUPPORT

Challenge yourself to stay dedicated to achieving your aspirational vision. Growth, like Visioneering, is a process. Certainly, be kind to yourself when life happens (kids, the bustle of everyday life, even pandemics), but be mindful to keep your vision work a priority. All too often, we sideline our big dreams and personal goals. To keep yourself accountable, form a professional support group.

Your support group members should be other strategic designers. It's important that everyone is playing at the same level. Set a recurring, monthly meeting. If your support group is local, perhaps you can coordinate meeting at a local restaurant or low-key bar. If not, schedule a virtual conference call. At each meeting, one of the members will act as a facilitator, while a handful of others present. Each presenter talks the group through the thin slice of their vision they are currently working on:

- What problem they are solving for?

- What's the hypothesis?

- What they are learning?

- How is it all going?

This line of questioning is similar to a Visioneering team's weekly review sessions and sprint demos. The group is there to offer critique, insights, brainstorm alternative ways of doing something, or lend a different perspective. The facilitator is there to guide the discussion to be kind, supportive and if possible, helpful. Sometimes, the best support can just be listening. Ultimately, support groups will be there to celebrate milestones of success, lend a helping hand through challenges, and importantly, motivate you to keep chipping away at your professional dreams.

AFTERWORD
PURPOSE DRIVEN

> There are professions more harmful than industrial design, but only a few of them. — VICTOR PAPANEK[1]

apanek was a designer, author, and activist who championed socially responsible design and teaching its real-world application. The message of his life's work is a reminder to strategic designers about the importance of wielding your newfound power responsibly. Designers and the companies that employ them have to be held accountable for the work they put out into the world. Sadly, not all companies strive to create a better world. So, if our goal as designers is to use our skillsets to leave a positive impact on society, the challenge becomes evaluating and choosing our employers wisely. *Purpose*, the underlying reason an action is taken, is your lens to assist with making that important decision. Purpose also adds meaning to your work and to your life. Maybe your purpose is

---

1 Victor Papanek, *Design for the Real World: Human Ecology and Social Change*

to be a world-famous designer or to join and build a start-up that goes public—making you a multimillionaire. Maybe you're focused on being a reliable provider for your family or being a great parent. Outside of family life, acclaim, and financial gain, purpose challenges you to clarify much bigger personal questions: What is your place in the world? What causes are you passionate about? How can you use your abilities as a designer to positively influence others and make the world a better place?

Knowing the answers to these questions will come in handy when you find yourself at life's crossroads or experiencing difficult times. Understanding your purpose will help you maintain perspective, focus on the task ahead, and serve as motivation because doing good, purposeful work has a chemical effect on your brain. That's right—our brains are naturally wired to thrive under these conditions, by way of happiness hormones. Remember the power of empathy? We used a well-told, empathic story to bond the stakeholder to the customer. That attachment is thanks to the hormone oxytocin. Its sibling, endorphins, are what cause a "helper's high," the rush that one feels after doing purposeful, good work. Mix the two together and that's a powerful concoction. It is especially effective when applied at the workplace and to your own professional development. It's a win-win for your employer and you.

SMALL ACTS OF GOOD

Not crystal clear on your purpose? Don't fret. It's never too late to jump on the purpose-driven train. Take the time now to investigate the issues and causes that mean the most to you and answer this bigger-than-life question. In the meantime, get to work creating purpose with small acts of good. You can accomplish this in your workplace by eliminating dark patterns and offering charitable pro bono hours.

DARK PATTERNS

Start by tackling what you can effectively change. As a design practitioner, draw a line in the sand. Don't tolerate design tactics that perpetuate manipulative marketing and sneaky sales practices. Examples include tricky questions, hidden costs, misdirection, and duplicitous tactics like confirmshaming, the act of insulting or guilting visitors into signing up for something. Sure, there may be some short-term gains for companies that manipulate their audience in this manner, but it certainly won't build a loyal fanbase who are excited to tell their friends and family about their great experience with your product. If you observe tactics that you consider devious and harmful to users where you work, speak up and demonstrate ways to improve the experience. If your employer isn't interested in the satisfaction of their customers, it's probably time to start looking for another job. This move will benefit your mental health—not to mention, any business that makes it a habit of pissing off its customers won't stay in business for long.

PRO BONO

Another way to get involved with purposeful work is to look to the non-profit sector, foundations, or charitable organizations. For these types of organizations, giving your time and expertise as a professional is more valuable than giving money. This pro bono (free of charge) work can often come with a title, such as board member or strategic adviser. Find the most appropriate fit for yourself by making a list of issues that you find mean-ingful—that is, what can you do to help make the world a better place. The next step is researching organizations aligned with your interests and sending inquiries out with information about your skills and how you may be able to help. Of those that move you, set up meetings with the executive directors or board members and share your pitch. You are looking to offer their organization pro bono work that leverages your unique strategic designer skillset. Perhaps the cause could greatly benefit from help with defining a vision for their service, clarifying their strategy, or applying Visioneering principles to their daily operation. You may have to recruit BEDRC volunteers occasionally for a Saturday's worth of work. Be prepared to put in more work up front, but once you are established and have some momentum with the team, you can cut back to 10 hours a month, plus monthly board meetings.

PURPOSE AND COMPANY ALIGNMENT

Do you already know what your purpose is? That's fantastic. Having a purpose that aligns with the mission of your organization is a key component of job satisfaction, success, and personal fulfillment. Your product vision isn't the only thing that is aligning with a company's North Star.

Consider the amount of time most of us spend at work. Forty hours per week? Fifty? Eighty? More? Many of us with full-time jobs spend more time with our colleagues than our own families. Frankly, some work long hours to escape their home life while many go to jobs that they don't particularly enjoy solely to support themselves and their families. If the place where you spend that much of your lifetime is, at best, just a paycheck or, at worst, a business that causes harm to the world through its products and services, it's time to reevaluate priorities. In the early 1980s when Apple was still a fledgling technology startup, Steve Jobs famously chided John Sculley in an effort to woo him to leave Pepsi and join Jobs at Apple: "Do you want to sell sugar water for the rest of your life, or do you want to come with me and change the world?" It worked.

Most of us can't afford to up and leave our jobs, and most of our work may never have the impact and reach of the products created by Apple. That doesn't mean that we, as design practitioners, can't make a positive impact on the world. Start by taking the time to examine your core values. Do those values align with the mission of the company where you work?

This may be a topic that you can check in on once or twice each year as your personal values and the missions of employers may gradually evolve. If you determine that you're out of alignment, consider two options: influence organizational change, or consider moving into a role that's a better fit with your values.

Be aware that organizational change is a tall order unless you have a considerable amount of influence at the highest level of the company. If executive leadership is committed to a mission that deviates from your personal values, you may be hard-pressed to realign their priorities. That doesn't mean you shouldn't try. Consider a pilot project—the same way you won the approval to prove the worth of your Visioneering endeavor. If you can convince the C-suite to use your strategic design skills to pursue a mission aligned with your passion and values, congratulations—you're back in business! Your work will be reinvigorated with a greater sense of purpose and meaning.

If you're unable to effect change within your current organization, take some time to start seeking out companies that are more complementary with your beliefs. There is no shortage of organizations that are in need of someone with your abilities to envision and deliver a better future for their customer base. Remember, when you find a place to work (or start one of your own) whose mission aligns with your own values, you will go to your job each day with a purpose and a level of engagement in the work that will motivate you beyond any salary and benefits package.

IN TIMES OF A PANDEMIC

The world has big, critical problems, begging to be solved—issues that harmfully affect the planet and its inhabitants on a global scale: climate change, hunger, poverty, COVID-19. In the midst of writing this book, the 2020 coronavirus pandemic wreaked havoc on the world. In a flash, everything changed. Where does the strategic designer fit in? The strategic designer's unique skillset (an innovative mindset, strategic prowess, and the ability to craft a clear and compelling vision) are vital to every company now. Every industry sector is being significantly affected by the pandemic: education, manufacturing, finance and insurance, food services, retail trade, transportation. Companies, large and small, are faced with the challenge to quickly recalibrate their current line of product and service offerings to serve the new way of the world. Those companies that embrace conservative ways over innovative ways will perish. Large corporations are particularly susceptible to falling back to traditional, conservative ways by slashing forward-thinking efforts to rely on the basics. If you work at one of these large companies, try persuading leadership to try the Visioneering way. Set up a conference call with your product program manager to discuss approval for the one to two weeks you and a small team will need to complete a pre-vision proposal. Hopefully, they will listen to you. Outside of your 9-to-5 job, there are the struggling mom-and-pop shops: the neighborhood coffee cafe, family-owned barbershop, local restaurant, and corner shop. To avoid extinction, your community's small businesses will need the strategic designer's help, too. Many of them are dying from the economic impacts of the pandemic but could be saved by transitioning (at least temporarily) to bring their services online. Another avenue a small business could consider alongside digitalization is to temporarily pivot. The strategic designer is a pro at identifying opportunities for a strategic pivot.

Here, help the small business stay true to their mission, but tweak the problem being solved and adjust the respective solution. For example, consider a local restaurant. A small restaurant could temporarily pivot to function as a pop-up shop that sells groceries. Pre-pandemic, any favorite local upscale restaurant focused on delivering the best of town sit-down dining experience. But with social distancing orders and states declaring lockdowns, a local restaurant is no longer open to patrons walking in to be seated for regular business. A simple research study would tell us the obvious: people are cutting back on non-essentials, which include eating out.

So, instead of offering the same fully cooked meals, via takeout and delivery, the restaurant could resell the wholesale food and goods they buy from their distributer. Hard-to-get household goods (think paper towels) are currently scarce at the grocery store and are in high demand. This type of clever pivot keeps a restaurant true to their mission and importantly, afloat during these uncertain times. Similar creative pivots could also apply to a local hairdresser or coffee shop.

To us strategic designers, change (big or small) is natural for us to wrap our heads around. But not so much for others. This may be especially true for a small business owner who have found longtime professional success abiding by convention (staying inside the box). In this case, they just need *permission* to think differently (leave the box). Grant that permission. Here's how to help: First, assemble a five-person BEDRC task force. Then call a local business manager or owner that you already have a relationship with—for example, the local coffee shop you used to frequent every morning before catching the commuter rail to the office. Offer one hour of your team's professional time to brainstorm how that small business owner could pivot or streamline their efforts to get up and running online. You could also recommend local business owners form meetups to share their learnings among each other. What types of innovative pivots are working? What's not? And importantly, why? Perhaps volunteer to occasionally help facilitate the meetup and drive the conversation. All of this help, while not asking much of the designer's time, grants business owners permission to think differently and embrace change. And that is invaluable to any local business owner attempting to weather uncertain times.

DESIGNING OUR FUTURE

The ability to define and execute a strategic product vision is key to any company weathering an economic crisis. But in times of need, vision work offers more than just a means of business survival. A vision is the embodiment of an optimistic, hopeful future. Visioneering provides the confidence there's always a way to strategically solve any problem and successfully navigate to that future. And today, who couldn't use some of that?

GLOSSARY

action What it will take to accomplish product initiatives. Examples of actions are services, product features, marketing campaigns, supplemental product offerings, and technical infrastructure.

agile development model An approach to project management where tasks are divided into short phases of work with frequent assessments and adjustments. This model is used most often, but not exclusively, in software development. Also referred to as *agile project management*.

BEDRC The "A-team" is made up of five key disciplines that will make your team the most effective. These are the BEDRC roles (pronounced "bedrock"): Business, Engineering, Design, Research, and Content. See Chapter 4, "Getting Started with the A-Team," page 84.

deliverables Tangible, documentary output created by a tactical designer.

elevated tactical designer An advanced tactical designer who elevates tactical efforts beyond design deliverables to contribute more making. The primary route to do this is to expand understanding of engineering and software development to become code savvy. The elevated tactical designer is the bridge that connects design to engineering. An elevated tactical designer is qualified to be a lead designer on scrum teams, and the best candidate to become a strategic designer, should they choose to pursue that route. See Chapter 1, "The State of the Designer," page 8.

experience pillars The most effective experiences are built on four universal experience pillars. These constitute the base from which a satisfying and valuable user experience is formed. Each pillar can be applied to any product or service in order to improve the overall customer journey.

> Pillar 1: Understand the customer's needs
> Pillar 2: Set expectations
> Pillar 3: Provide value
> Pillar 4: Measure results

See Chapter 6, " Telling the Story of the Future Experience," page 154.

experience story Also referred to as the *story of the experience*. This is the heart of a product vision. The structure of the experience story leverages traditional storytelling elements but with a unique spin, for example mapping scenes to the four experience pillars. The story explains the strategy's complex connections by communicating of the future state of the user's experience. See Chapter 6, "Telling the Story of the Future Experience," page 157.

first principles Measurable and proven truths or fundamental laws of nature. See Chapter 3, "Master Class: First Principles Thinking," page 60.

first principles thinking Involves identifying and challenging assumptions and breaking down problems into their component parts to truly understand them. See Chapter 3, "Master Class: First Principles Thinking."

hypothesis A proposed explanation based on limited evidence. A supposition used as a starting point, to be supported or contradicted by further investigation.

modern-era design Practitioners of modern-era design are called on to be skilled in defining not only form and function, but strategy as well. Designers adept at modern-era design leverage their highly creative lenses to assemble connections via skillful problem solving. With this new platform, designers can envision and create the future—a gift that brings a weighty responsibility. We must use this gift to its fullest extent and effect change only for the *better*. See Chapter 1, "The State of the Designer," page 27.

MVP In product development, the initials MVP are understood to stand for *minimum viable product*. For our purposes, alternate words for the letters MVP will help guide the Visioneering process. Instead of a minimum viable product, think of your MVP as an experiment—the *Means of Validating a hyPothesis*. With your team's well-defined objectives and hypothesis, define the MVP experiment that the team will create to validate that hypothesis. See Chapter 7, "Setting Your Compass to the North Star," page 203.

North Star A company's mission and purpose—their raison d'être. All of a company's products and services should align with their North Star.

pairing An agile/scrum practice in which a developer and designer work side by side on a sprint story, coding and designing in real time.

pivot A seismic shift to a product vision. This will happen during the delivery phase. When a team encounters a need to pivot, the execution is paused, and the team falls back to the product vision process, phase 2 (strategy). The strategy is modified, the experience story changed, and the prototype updated accordingly. The team again validates the entire body of work with both executive stakeholders and customers. Only then, when the pivot (adjusted product vision) is accepted, can Visioneering resume. See Chapter 7, "Setting Your Compass to the North Star," page 209.

product vision The product vision is the keystone of any product or service. The goal of a product vision is to explain a strategy's complex connections and express the product's future intended destination. This can be done by telling the story of an experience (the heart of a product vision) and conceptually illustrating the offering's intentions, without getting into detailed designing. Ultimately, our product vision conveys the story of how our product or service will forge an idealized partnership between the company and their customer. Think of it as the overarching game plan that fuses a bold future with thoughtful strategy and clearly reflects the values of an organization. It should enable a product team to achieve greatness. At the end of the process a product vision is a stand-alone deliverable—capable of demonstrating clear and inspirational future ambitions for a product or service without the need to include additional explanation. Part II, "The Vision."

product vision deficit A product or service without a strategy-led product vision. Offerings that have product vision deficit have telltale red flags, including a lack of clear business objectives, vaguely addressed user problems, and misalignment with the company's mission. See Chapter 4, "Getting Started with the A-Team," page 78.

prototype A testable, early-stage release of a product, service, or process that you want to build. Importantly, a prototype is not fully functioning or high-fidelity.

remix A new concept created by modifying someone else's idea or melding concepts from multiple presenters. One concept can build on and augment another concept for the better.

scrum Used in agile development, scrums emphasize daily communication, teamwork and short, iterative phases of work. This ties into the flexibility of plans that characterize the agile approach.

sprint A continuous development cycle is comprised of sprints. A sprint is a timeboxed increment that can be one, two- or three-weeks long. Within a sprint, the aim is for a scrum team to complete the planned amount of work and be ready for review by the end of the allocated time.

stakeholder Refers to an individual who sponsors a product vision endeavor and Visioneering expedition. At a company this is likely senior leadership, an executive, or senior business partner.

strategic building blocks The five strategic building blocks are the where, the who, the what, the when, and the why. During the strategy phase, teams work sequentially through each of the five building blocks, and go back as needed, until a solid foundation exists. For our purposes, if the product vision is the keystone of any product or service, your strategy is the masonry. Masonry is the craft of making a solid whole out of components. All components must fit together and interlock. The product vision, your keystone, will be the central element that locks and secures the strategic building blocks in place. See Chapter 5, "Strategy: Connecting the Dots," page 103.

strategy The overarching, high-level game plan that connects the dots and defines major goals and objectives (distinguished from tactics, which accomplish objectives in service of the strategy).

strategic designer The practitioner of modern-era design. They lead product vision efforts and co-captain Visioneering endeavors as a member of the triad. They form a bridge that connects design to business, as well as design and engineering.

tactic A task or step that works to accomplish actions and initiatives in the service of an overall strategy. Can also refer to such an action in general, not in context of a project; for example, a tactic in the toolbox that is available if needed.

tactical designer A designer who works to deliver tactical deliverables. Responsibilities include writing hypotheses, clarifying user problems, identifying potential usability concerns and defining form and function by creating visuals, visual languages, design systems, and information architecture.

timeboxed Where a limit is set on the time to be allocated to a task or phase.

triad At the heart of the Visioneering team structure is the triad. The triad includes the champions of the product vision and the leaders of the Visioneering process. The three members of a triad are the B, E, and D of BEDRC: the product manager (B), the technology head (E) and the strategic designer (D). Every product vision must have a triad in place—no exceptions! The triad ensures that the teams are working independently toward delivering their respective actions while sharing what they've learned, coordinating, and collaborating on achieving the broader product vision. See Chapter 7, "Setting Your Compass to the North Star," page 200.

trial product vision For companies that want to test drive this new way of approaching product work. A trial period is comprised of one full product vision endeavor, and the time required to complete all four phases of the product vision process. At the end of the trial, stakeholders decide whether to adopt strategy-led product vision and Visioneering as an accepted way of working. A trial product vision moves forward into Visioneering.

Visioneering A new approach that resurrects the practice of developing and aligning teams to the achievement of a product vision. Today, every product or service journey is an uncharted expedition. Now more than ever, the landscape is unpredictable—quick to change due to the fast-paced nature of technology and ever-rising bar of user expectations. What the team sees in front of them now may soon shift, rendering product roadmaps obsolete. To help us maneuver this terrain, we can use Visioneering as a navigational tool to execute our product vision while keeping in alignment with the North Star (the company's mission and purpose). Visioneering ensures that the product is bound to a purposeful direction as the team iteratively and continuously delivers the best experience that meets the needs of both the business and the target audience.

working agreements Agreements are commonly used on agile teams and represent how team members arrange to work with one another. These agreements often include times of day when team members are available to meet versus when they're actively working; communication standards. For example: use video if meeting remotely or document new research findings in the team Slack channel. They also include general rules of engagement for how to productively interact and work with one another.

workshop A working session that is often a full day or half day, where a team works to accomplish a predefined objective. Workshop facilitation requires a keen ability for managing group dynamics, the ability to adapt and improvise, proficiency with active listening, and consensus building.

INDEX

CREDITS

ICONS

Figures on pages 22-23, 32, 37, 50, 85, 94, 97, 102, 107, 116, 132, 155, 164, 182-183, 190, 191, 193, 194, 197, 199, 215, 218, and 225 contain icons from M.Style/Shutterstock.

Microphone icon on pages xxiv, 26, 41, 90, and 227 by Aleksandr Naim/Shutterstock.

QUOTES

Note: Page numbers refer to where quote appears in this book.

Page 11. Robert F. Kennedy, Jr.

Page 27. Joseph Campbell, *The Hero's Journey: Joseph Campbell on His Life and Work* (Novato, CA: New World Library, 2014).

Page 143. Upton Sinclair, *I, Candidate for governor: and how I got licked,* California, 1935.

Page 153. Don Norman and Jakob Nielsen, *The Definition of User Experience (UX)*, Nielsen Norman Group.

Page 232. Papanek, Victor J, *Design for the real world: human ecology and social change*, New York: Pantheon Books, 1973.

Page 235. Steve Jobs, to Pepsi executive John Sculley.